The Great
Irish Famine

MILESTONES
IN MODERN
WORLD HISTORY

The Boer War

The Bolshevik
Revolution

The British
Industrial Revolution

The Chinese
Cultural Revolution

The Collapse of
the Soviet Union

The Congress of Vienna

The Cuban Revolution

D-Day and the
Liberation of France

The End of Apartheid
in South Africa

The Establishment
of the State of Israel

The French Revolution
and the Rise
of Napoleon

The Great Irish Famine

The Indian
Independence
Act of 1947

The Iranian Revolution

The Manhattan Project

The Marshall Plan

The Mexican
Revolution

The Treaty of Nanking

The Treaty of Versailles

The Universal
Declaration of
Human Rights

MILESTONES
IN MODERN
WORLD HISTORY

1600 · · · 1750 · ·

· · · 1940 · · · 2000

The Great Irish Famine

LIZ SONNEBORN

CHELSEA HOUSE
An Infobase Learning Company

The Great Irish Famine

Chelsea House
An imprint of Infobase Learning
132 West 31st Street
New York, NY 10001

Library of Congress Cataloging-in-Publication Data

Sonneborn, Liz.
The great Irish famine / by Liz Sonneborn.
    p. cm. — (Milestones in modern world history)
Includes bibliographical references and index.
ISBN 978-1-60413-918-1 (hardcover)
1. Ireland—History—Famine, 1845–1852—Juvenile literature. 2. Famines—Ireland—History—19th century—Juvenile literature. I. Title. II. Series.
DA950.7.S67 2011
941.5081—dc22   2011011607

Chelsea House books are available at special discounts when purchased in bulk quantities for businesses, associations, institutions, or sales promotions. Please call our Special Sales Department in New York at (212) 967-8800 or (800) 322-8755.

You can find Chelsea House on the World Wide Web at http://www.infobaselearning.com.

Text design by Erik Lindstrom
Cover design by Alicia Post
Composition by Keith Trego
Cover printed by Yurchak Printing, Landisville, Pa.
Book printed and bound by Yurchak Printing, Landisville, Pa.
Printed in the United States of America

CONTENTS

Skibbereen

In the early weeks of 1847, James Mahony left London, England, and set out for western Ireland. Mahony was a well-known artist, particularly acclaimed for his watercolors of city scenes. But it was his talent as an illustrator that convinced the editors of the *Illustrated London News*—one of the most popular newspapers in England—to send him to Ireland on assignment. As the paper's name implies, much of its success was due to its engraved illustrations, which in an era before photographs, provided readers with a visual image of what its reporters described in words.

The *News* asked Mahony to investigate a series of reports that were coming out of the Irish county of Cork. Since the autumn of 1845, Ireland had been experiencing food shortages because of the failure of its potato crop. Among the poor of Ireland, the potato was the most important source of food. Though Ireland had suffered from lean potato harvests in the past, the news coming from County Cork suggested that the famine was far more serious this time.

DR. DONOVAN'S DIARY

The *Illustrated London News* had already reprinted some reports that had first appeared in the *Cork Southern Reporter*. They were written by Daniel Donovan, a respected physician who was devoted to caring for the poor in rural Ireland. In printed excerpts from his *Diary of a Dispensary Doctor*, Donovan—known as Dr. Dan to his patients—described the horrors the famine was inflicting on the town of Skibbereen, located at the southwestern tip of Ireland. Day in and day out, Donovan attended to Skibbereen's ill and dying. Its people were not only plagued by starvation, but were also suffering from epidemic disease during the coldest winter in recent memory. The conditions in Skibbereen were almost unimaginably terrible, even for the experienced doctor. As Donovan wrote, "[T]hough rendered callous by a companionship for many years with disease and death, . . . I was completely unnerved at the humble seen [*sic*] of suffering and misery that was presented to my view."[1]

One of the stories Donovan told was about the Barrett family. The Barretts, evicted from their house and farm, were living in an abandoned guardhouse in a cemetery. Outside the tiny house were piles of rotting bodies, which no one dared to bury out of fear of disease. When Donovan looked inside the house, he saw that six members of the family "males and females, labouring under most malignant fever, were huddled together, as closely as were the dead in graves around."[2] He was nearly overwhelmed by the awful stench emanating from their dying bodies.

When Donovan entered, the Barretts called out, "Is that the Priest? Is that the Doctor?"[3] They all begged him for something to drink. He had brought tea and sugar with him, but

Ireland

ATLANTIC OCEAN

SCOTLAND (U.K.)

North Channel

Aran Island
Dungloe
Letterkenny
Gweebarra Bay
Lough Swilly

Donegal

NORTHERN IRELAND (U.K.)

Donegal Bay

Inisfree Island
Sligo

Monaghan

Blacksod Bay
Achill I.
Clare Island
Lough Conn
Ballina

Cavan
Dundalk
Carlingford Lough
Irish Sea

Clew Bay
Castlebar
Knock
Carrick on Shannon
Erne

Lough Mask
Roscommon
Longford
Blackwater R.
Boyne R.
Drogheda

Lough Ree

Clifden
Lough Corrib
Mullingar

Galway
Ballinasloe
Athlone
Clonmacnoise
Tullamore
Shannon R.
Liffey R.
Dun Laoghaire
Dublin
Bray

Aran Islands
Galway Bay
Gort
Portlaoise
Wicklow

Lough Derg
Castledermot

Ennis
Nenagh
Carlow
Arklow
Barrow R.
Bann R.

Limerick
Kilkenny

Listowel
Tipperary
Cashel
Clonmel
Nore R.
New Ross

Tralee
Newmarket
Waterford
Suir R.
Wexford

Blasket Islands
Dingle
Killorglin
Killarney
Blackwater R.
Dungarvan
Saltee Islands

Dingle Bay
Blarney
Cork
St. George's Channel

Valentia I.
Kenmare
Lee R.
Youghal
Cobh

Kenmare Bay
Kinsale
Bantry
Ballinspittle
N

Bear I.
Bantry Bay

Clear Island

| 0 | 50 miles |
| 0 | 50 km |

© Infobase Learning

The potato famine that devastated Ireland between 1845 and 1852 did not affect the entire nation in the same way. Leinster and Ulster escaped the worst ravages of the famine, while suffering was greater in western Ireland, particularly Connacht, and in the west of Munster.

he realized they had no fire, even though a storm of wind and cold rain raged outside. The family was happy with the bread and water he offered, which probably allowed them to survive the night. Donovan arranged for the Barretts to be taken to the hospital, where he reported that their health was improving. But as his descriptions of the corpses littering the fields and streets revealed, many people of Skibbereen were not so lucky as to have a savior like Donovan reach them in their most desperate hour of need.

A MOTHER'S SORROW

Though Donovan was a medical expert and a leading authority on death by famine, many readers had trouble believing his stories. They may have accepted that the potato shortage was dire in Ireland, but surely Donovan and other writers of similar tales had to be exaggerating the situation in Skibbereen. After all, since 1801 Ireland had been part of the United Kingdom of Great Britain and Ireland, then the most prosperous country in the world. It seemed impossible that this scale of want and hunger could occur in such a rich nation.

To satisfy its skeptical readers, the *Illustrated London News* sent James Mahony to provide an eyewitness account, in words and pictures, of exactly what was going on in Skibbereen and the surrounding area. In addition to his drawing skills, Mahony had been born in Cork and knew the area well. The paper's editors felt his background would make him a reliable correspondent. Cork was such a poor area that, even in a time of a healthy harvest, the living conditions might alarm a stranger to the region. As the editors explained, Mahony "must already have been somewhat familiar with such scenes of suffering in his own locality, so that he cannot be supposed to have taken an *extreme* view of the greater misery at Skibbereen."[4]

Mahony's experiences in Ireland were recounted in two articles published on February 13 and 20, 1847. His story began as he set off west from Cork, the largest city in County Cork.

His stagecoach made a stop in the small town of Clonakilty. It was there that Mahony first saw the toll the famine was taking on the Irish. Clonakilty's poorest, all begging for money to buy food, immediately mobbed the coach. One woman in the crowd attracted Mahony's attention. In his sketch of the woman, her expression betrayed her intense sorrow, which was further revealed by the dead infant she cradled in her arms. She begged for coins like the others, but she wanted money for a coffin in which to bury her baby.

Moved by the woman's plight, Mahony asked about her at a local hotel. The proprietor said she was far from unique. Every day, dozens of people arrived in town with similar stories of grief and suffering.

"THE MISERY AND HORROR"

"After leaving Clonakilty," Mahony wrote, "each step that we took westward brought fresh evidence of the truth of the reports of the misery."[5] Along the road, he saw funeral after funeral. The sheer number of funerals was upsetting, but even more disturbing was the fact that few people attended. At most, there were about 10 people at each funeral; at others, only one or two. The Irish had had a long tradition of celebrating a loved one's life when he or she died. This new seeming indifference to death startled Mahony and convinced him that this famine was unlike any other.

His worst fears were confirmed when he reached Skibbereen. In his report, Mahony admitted that he had questioned Donovan's writings because he thought the doctor was creating "highly-coloured pictures" for the "good and humane purpose" of encouraging charities to help the suffering Irish. "[B]ut," Mahony wrote, "I can now, with perfect confidence, say that neither pen nor pencil ever could portray the miser[y] and horror, at this moment, to be witnessed in Skibbereen."[6] He explained that "not a single house out of 500 could boast of being free from death and fever."[7]

WOMAN BEGGING AT CLONAKILTY.

In this 1847 illustration by James Mahony, a woman with a baby begs at Clonakilty in County Cork during the Irish famine. Approximately a million people died from starvation and disease and another million fled as immigrants to Great Britain and North America during the famine years.

The elderly and sickly were not the only ones dying in large numbers. Starvation and disease were also killing the young and vigorous. Mahony wrote about accompanying Dr. Donovan to "one house, without door or window, filled with destitute people lying on the bare floor."[8] Among them was a "fine, tall, stout country lad, who had entered some hours previously to find shelter from the piercing cold, [who] lay here dead amongst others likely soon to follow him."[9] The people in the house begged for Mahony's help, but Donovan made him wait outside while he tended to them, for fear that Mahony himself would fall victim to disease.

In nearby Schull, Mahony saw hundreds of women line up to buy food from agents of the British government. The only food they offered was cornmeal imported from the United States. This type of corn, called Indian corn, was very hard to digest. In better times, the Irish would have considered it too foul to eat, but now each woman was desperate to get the measly portions the agents sold at prices they could scarcely afford. One woman told Mahony she had been in line since dawn. Yet she and the others with her were determined to wait as long as needed to make sure that their families had at least something to eat that day.

NO END IN SIGHT

During his stay, Mahony was eager to investigate one story told by Donovan that had particularly disturbed his paper's readers. Donovan claimed that after a man named Leahey died, his wife and two children, seeking shelter from the cold, stayed in the house with his corpse. Finally, however, the smell of the body drove them outside. A few days later, people passing by the house heard a snarling noise inside. Peering in, they saw a pack of hungry dogs eating Leahey's body.

Mahony sought out Reverend J. Creedon, who had ministered to Leahey and "prepared the man for death."[10] Creedon and a neighbor of Leahey not only confirmed Donovan's story but also revealed that "the case was even more disgusting than there stated."[11] It was not passersby who came upon the gruesome scene, but Leahey's own mother who had found the animals ripping his corpse to shreds.

A visit to the relatively "large and thriving"[12] town of Dunmanway to the east seemed to provide a respite from scenes of misery. But Mahony noticed that even in Dunmanway, there appeared to be an "entire abandonment of agricul-

"REVENGE FOR SKIBBEREEN"

The famine era inspired a folk song titled "Skibbereen." Its lyrics in the version below recount a conversation between an Irish father and son, who now live in an unspecified place far from Ireland. The boy asks his father why they left Skibbereen when he was only two. The father explains how, unable to pay his rent and taxes, he and his family were evicted from their home. After his wife died, he said goodbye to Skibbereen and emigrated from Ireland with the boy. The song ends on a defiant note, with the boy vowing to fight for Irish independence from British rule. "Revenge for Skibbereen" remains a popular song among contemporary Irish musicians. In recent years, it has been recorded by Sinead O'Connor, the Wolfe Tones, and The Dubliners.

> Oh son, I loved my native land with energy and pride
> Till a blight came o'er the praties [potatoes]; my sheep, my
>   cattle died
> My rent and taxes went unpaid, I could not them redeem
> And that's the cruel reason why I left old Skibbereen.

tural occupation."[13] He saw very few fields that were ready for planting in the spring, evidence that the famine was sure to continue well into the future. Mahony learned that farmers saw little reason to plant a new potato crop. Even if the crop were not infected by the disease that had destroyed the previous two harvests, "the poor famished wretches would be there to eat them [the potato tubers] up long before they had time to grow."[14]

Oh well do I remember that bleak December day
The landlord and the sheriff came to take us all away
They set my roof on fire with their cursed English spleen
I heaved a sigh and bade goodbye to dear old Skibbereen.

Your mother too, God rest her soul, fell on the stony ground
She fainted in her anguish seeing desolation 'round
She never rose but passed away from life to immortal dream
She found a quiet grave, me boy, in dear old Skibbereen.

And you were only two years old and feeble was your frame
I could not leave you with my friends for you bore your
    father's name
I wrapped you in my cota mor [overcoat] in the dead of night
    unseen
I heaved a sigh and bade goodbye to dear old Skibbereen.

Oh father dear, the day will come when in answer to the call
All Irish men of freedom stern will rally one and all
I'll be the man to lead the band beneath the flag of green
And loud and clear we'll raise the cheer, Revenge for
    Skibbereen.*

* "Skibbereen." Moving Here: Migration Histories. http:// www.movinghere.org.uk/galleries/histories/irish/origins/ skibbereen_1.htm.

One of the most moving sketches Mahony created to accompany his article was of a boy and girl he had met on the road. With the dulled eyes of the dying, they looked out at the reader as they desperately dug in the dirt, in search of a potato all the other starving scavengers might have missed. Behind them, Mahony wrote, was a pile of six bodies, which the children seemed not to notice.

A PLEA FOR HELP

Having every moment of their lives consumed by thoughts of death, the Irish people Mahony met displayed a callousness toward the dead that deeply disturbed him. He especially noted the hardheartedness of the men who transported coffins to church cemeteries: "I saw one of them, with four coffins in a car, driving to the churchyard, sitting upon one of the said coffins, and smoking with much apparent enjoyment."[15]

A mere visitor to the disaster, Mahony could not turn off his emotions so easily. In one of his final sketches, he drew the interior of a hut where a man named Mullins lay dying on a mound of straw. His three children, ignoring their father, crouched around a fire, Mahony's editors wrote, "as if to raise the last remaining spark of life."[16] In the middle of the picture, Mahony showed the local vicar, seated in a chair, the dirt on the floor up to his ankles as he observed Mullins in his final hours. The quiet contrast between the miserable family in rags and the vicar in his suit and top hat echoed the gulf between the suffering Irish and the outside world, where few could imagine the horrors that had become a part of their everyday life.

Mahony ended his story with a desperate plea: "I entreat you to do the best you can for so much suffering humanity; as this visit to the West will, I trust, assist in making this affliction known to the charitable public."[17]

MEMORIES OF FAMINE

Mahony's articles were just two among many reports that helped spread news of the disaster in Ireland not just to Britain but also to the United States, Canada, and beyond. Mahony's articles, however, were the ones that particularly struck a nerve with readers. His sketches depicted the suffering of the Irish in a way that made it impossible for anyone to look away. The drawings are still among the most famous images of the disaster now known as the Great Irish Famine.

As public awareness grew, people from around the world offered charity to Ireland. But even with this aid, relief efforts fell far short of what was needed. The famine, which lasted for five dark years, was one of the most terrible humanitarian disasters of the nineteenth century. Although the precise number of dead remains unknown, an estimated one million—one-eighth of Ireland's population—died during the famine years. At least another million left the country, most for good.

The famine changed Ireland and its people forever. Still today, more than a century and a half later, tales of the era's deprivation and degradation remain fresh in the psyche of the Irish. The Great Irish Famine also continues to be the subject of controversy and debate. Was the mass suffering the inevitable result of a natural disaster? Or did their more fortunate British countrymen shamelessly exploit the famine in order to grind down the Irish?

Before the Famine

In the early 1840s, about 8 million people lived in Ireland. While some lived in growing cities such as Dublin and Belfast, most Irish lived in the countryside. Nearly two-thirds of all Irish people made their living through farming.

Most farmland in Ireland was owned by a small group of landlords. Their large estates had been passed down through many generations. Although most landlords were Irish, many lived in England, far from their landholdings. They came to think of themselves more as Englishmen than as Irishmen. They also adopted the lavish lifestyles of rich English landowners, which often required them to take on a daunting amount of debt.

LANDLORDS AND TENANTS

Many landlords were uninterested in managing their property themselves. Instead, they hired agents to lease their lands and collect rent. The landlords did not care who leased their estates as long the rent money kept pouring in. They also made few improvements to their landholdings. In their eyes, their estates were there to make them income, not to cost them money. On the landlords' behalf, agents tried to squeeze the highest rents possible out of the tenants. If a tenant seemed to have any extra income, an agent might raise the rent or send a bailiff to evict the tenant so the plot could be rented out at a higher rate. As one visitor to Ireland explained, "the putting on a new coat, the addition of a trifling article of furniture, or the appearance of anything like comfort in or around his [a tenant's] dwelling was a sure and certain notice that the bailiff would be 'down upon him' ere the sun had set."[1]

Large properties were usually broken up into smaller farms. Some measured more than 20 acres (8.09 hectacres), but most were fewer than 10 acres (4.04 ha). If the harvest was good, a farmer leasing one of these plots could earn enough to feed his family, pay his rent, and pay taxes levied by the county, but not much more. On the eve of the Great Irish Famine, small farmers were becoming slightly more prosperous. But their annual income was tiny in comparison to what landlords made each year in rents.

Small farmers usually grew grain, which they exported to England. They relied on poor laborers to do much of the farm work. In exchange, the farmers gave laborers a little plot that they could farm to feed their families. Laborers sometimes also raised livestock.

EKING OUT A LIVING

Though a few Irish landlords lived in grand mansions on their estates, most people in rural Ireland had very modest dwellings with mud walls, clay floors, and thatched roofs. The mud house of those who were a bit better off might have several rooms and windows. The homes of poorer workers, however, usually featured just one windowless room with a hole in the roof to release smoke from a cooking fire.

Many poor Irish did not even have that. Migrant workers who traveled from place to place in search of temporary seasonal work, they often spent several months out of the year in England and Scotland, where they brought in the yearly harvest for low wages. People who could not find any work at all congregated in towns and cities, where they eked out a miserable existence by begging.

The very poor did have one alternative: They could go to live in a workhouse. In 1834, Parliament, the lawmaking body

INDUSTRY AND AGRICULTURE

By the mid-nineteenth century, England was rapidly becoming industrialized. New machinery and steam power allowed factories to create mass-produced goods that would come to replace items previously made by hand.

The Industrial Revolution that was transforming England, however, largely passed Ireland by. In part, this was due to Ireland's lack of mineral resources, most notably coal, which was burned as fuel to power factories.

Not only did Ireland remain an agricultural nation, it also relied on less efficient agricultural technology. In England, farm owners could afford to use the latest farming equipment and modern agricultural techniques, which helped increase their yields.

Ireland, in contrast, was burdened by a complicated system of land ownership and leasing. Large landowners controlled farmland that, often through middlemen, was broken up and leased to many different farmers. The farmers then in turn broke up their farmland to provide the laborers they hired with their own small plots to sustain their families. As the Irish population grew and people began marry-

of Britain and Ireland, passed the Poor Law Amendment Act, which called for the establishment of a network of workhouses to aid the poverty-stricken. By 1845, there were about 125 such workhouses in Ireland.

British politicians did not want to encourage the poor to seek aid from the government. Many believed the poor were poor because they were lazy. As a result, the lawmakers who wrote the Poor Law went out of their way to make sure that life in the government-operated workhouses was as unpleasant as possible.

ing earlier, landholdings were further subdivided. Families often gave a portion of their lands to newly married couples, making it harder for each family to grow enough food to feed themselves. In addition, agricultural workers in Ireland were generally very poor. They considered themselves lucky if they possessed simple farming implements, such as a hoe or a spade.

Contrary to the way they were popularly portrayed by the English, poor Irish farm workers were extremely industrious. As one observer noted, "I have never seen any field cultivation in England, except perhaps hops, where more diligence is discovered [than in growing potatoes in Ireland]. Every ounce of manure is carefully husbanded, and every weed is destroyed. The drainage is made complete; and the hoe, or rather the apology for that instrument [the spade], is constantly going."*

Yet, the Irish system of landownership and Ireland's widespread poverty inhibited the development of its agricultural economy. By the time of the Great Irish Famine, the productivity of the average agricultural worker in Ireland was only half what it was in England.

* James S. Donnelly, *The Great Irish Potato Famine*. Stroud, Gloucestershire: Sutton, 2001, p. 9.

This period photograph from Achill Island depicts the type of cabins that were common in Ireland during the years of the Irish famine. At the time, most Irish lived on subsistence farms.

Everyone in the workhouse, except for the very young and the very ill, had to labor for many hours a day, often working at extremely boring tasks. Men had to break stones or grind corn. Women had to wash linen and scrub floors. In the workhouse, the poor also had to obey a long series of rules meant to teach them self-discipline. They could be punished if they refused to work, used vulgar language, or spoke with one another during meals. The famous English writer Charles Dickens memorably depicted such drudgery in his 1838 novel *Oliver Twist*, in which the title character, a poor orphan, is sent to live in a workhouse.

Not surprisingly, few people were willing to admit them-selves into a workhouse. Most of the desperately poor preferred to live on the streets and beg for a living.

DEPENDING ON THE POTATO

Despite rampant poverty, the population of Ireland grew dra-matically during the early nineteenth century. In 1800, there were about 5 million people in Ireland. Just 40 years later, that number had grown to about 8 million. The population of other areas in Europe grew during this time, but not at this high rate. Additionally, the population did not explode uniformly throughout Ireland. The greatest population jumps occurred in the south and the west, the poorest areas of Ireland.

While the population rose in Ireland, so did the popularity of a particular food—the potato. Some scholars argue that the increase in potato farming led to the increase in population, as potatoes were a very cheap and plentiful food source that allowed people to feed large families. Other experts, however, contend that the population boom came first. They theorize that the Irish people began planting more potatoes to feed their already growing numbers.

The potato was not native to Ireland. It originated in the Americas and was introduced to Ireland in about 1590. The country's mild and damp climate proved ideal for growing the plant. Potatoes were eventually farmed throughout Europe, but no population grew as dependent on potatoes as the Irish. In the early 1840s, the average poor man in Ireland ate from 12 to 14 pounds of potatoes a day. The diet of about 3 million people in Ireland consisted almost entirely of potatoes.

Most diets limited largely to a single food would lead to malnutrition. The potato, however, is extremely rich in vitamins and nutrients. Even poor Irish people could usually supplement their diet with a little milk or buttermilk, which helped make up for the few nutrients lacking in their staple food. In fact, the

This illustration of an Irish cabin shows its inhabitants with their potato store over their heads. Though not a native product of Ireland, the potato became central to the Irish diet in the decades leading up the famine.

eating habits of the Irish poor were so conducive to health that the average Irishman was taller than the average Englishman.

INCREASING THE POTATO HARVEST

Potatoes also became popular in Ireland because they were extremely easy to grow. Growing grains such as oats, barley, and wheat required farmers to prepare fields laboriously. Seed potatoes, on the other hand, could just be dropped in dirt broken up by spades and then covered with earth. To make sure the potato plants thrived, farmers fertilized potato beds with seaweed or animal manure. Laborers with even the smallest plots, therefore, tried to raise at least one pig. The pig ate potatoes, then produced the manure needed to grow even more potatoes. Grown pigs could be sold for cash that poor families used to buy necessities, such as clothing for their children.

As the demand for farmland to grow potatoes grew, so did prices for premium plots. People started looking for plots of unused land to farm. For the first time, they tried cultivating hillsides and bogs, which were areas of wet, muddy ground. With enough manure, the hearty potato plant could flourish even in these previously unproductive areas. Especially in the south and west, poor Irish farmers and laborers created all-new bog villages during the first decades of the nineteenth century.

To increase the potato harvest, the Irish also began growing a variety called horse potatoes, or lumpers. Watery lumpers were less tasty and nutritious than other types of potatoes. They also were less resistant to disease. But they grew well in bad soil and reliably delivered higher yields. As more and more families relied almost exclusively on the potato for their survival, the benefit of a fairly dependable harvest outweighed any drawbacks.

DOING WITHOUT

For the people dependent on potatoes, even a good harvest did not ensure that they would have enough food to eat year-round. Potatoes were planted in April and May. They were ready for harvest beginning in late August. The bulk of the harvested potatoes were then stored in pits for later use.

For most people, however, their potato stores began to run dry in May. Therefore, there were about three difficult months between the time the potatoes from the previous harvest were gone to the time the potatoes from the next harvest were ready to eat. Poor Irish had to scramble to survive what they called the summer hunger. If they were lucky, the farmer who leased them their potato plot might provide them some help. Or they might have a pig to sell to get them enough money to buy oatmeal or corn. If they were not lucky, they might have to beg strangers for enough food or money just to keep alive from day to day.

In addition to the summer hunger, the Irish were accustomed to the occasional crop failure. An overly rainy year would waterlog the potato plants and cause them to rot while still in ground. An overly dry year could prevent the plants from growing at all. Also, from time to time, potato harvests were destroyed by disease, such as those popularly known as the curl and dry rot. Whether caused by weather or disease, partial crop failures led to a series of famines in Ireland during the early nineteenth century; the worst ones occurred in 1815, 1822, 1826, and 1831. Although many people suffered and some people died in each famine, short-term government relief and private charity in each case helped minimize the misery experienced by the Irish. Even more important, each lean year affected only a portion of the potato crop and lasted for only one growing season. Through the summer hunger and partial crop failures, the Irish had long been familiar with times of trouble and need. Unfortunately, even these trying times could not prepare them for the large-scale horror the Great Irish Famine would visit upon them.

The Blight

O n September 9, 1845, the *Dublin Evening Post* reported that the potato crop had failed "very extensively in the United States, to a great extent in Flanders and France, and to an appreciable amount in England."[1] For most readers, this was old news. Since June, they had heard that something was attacking the potato crop in several European countries, including France, Germany, Switzerland, and the Netherlands. Potatoes contaminated by what came to be known as the blight turned black, mushy, and rotten. In August, the Irish learned that the blight had attacked the potato crop in southern England as well. The *Post* knew its readership was worried about the blight and promised to collect all information it could about whether or not it might reach Ireland.

The newspaper story, however, concluded on a positive note: "[H]appily, there is no ground for any apprehensions of the kind in Ireland. There may have been partial failures in some localities; but, we believe that there was never a more abundant potato crop in Ireland than there is at present."[2]

Only four days later, a report in the *Gardeners' Chronicle*, an English horticultural journal, destroyed any hope that the blight might bypass Ireland: "We stop the Press, with very great regret, to announce that the POTATO MURRAIN has unequivocally declared itself in Ireland. The crops about Dublin are suddenly perishing." The article then asked a horrifying question that anyone who read those words were already anxiously asking themselves: "[W]here will Ireland be, in the event of a universal Potato rot?"[3]

ASSESSING THE CRISIS

Even with that question looming, many people in Ireland remained optimistic. After all, more farmland was being cultivated in Ireland than ever before, so if the damage caused by the blight was limited, the entire harvest might be enough to prevent mass starvation. Many were also buoyed by the grain harvest. By autumn, it was clear that Ireland would see a bumper oat crop.

In October, though, as farm laborers dug up the latest potatoes in their harvest, everyone became alarmed. The blackened potatoes they pulled from the ground were evidence that the blight had indeed spread throughout Ireland. Fear turned to panic as many of the seemingly healthy potatoes that Irish farmers had stored earlier began to rot.

Among those most upset by the news from Ireland was Sir Robert Peel. As prime minister, he was the head of the government of the United Kingdom of Great Britain and Ireland. Peel was well familiar with the Irish and their dependence on the potato. During the partial potato crop failure of 1816–1817, he had served as the government's chief secretary for Ireland. In

As prime minister of Great Britain in the first years of the Irish famine, Sir Robert Peel oversaw a concerted government effort to combat it. He is also remembered for creating the modern concept of the police force. Today, officers are known as "bobbies" in England and "Peelers" in Ireland after Peel.

this capacity, he arranged for £250,000 of government funds to be spent for relief to the Irish poor. His actions helped contain the suffering caused by the near famine conditions.

On October 15, 1845, Peel wrote to Lord Heytesbury, an official in Ireland, asking for more information about what was happening. Heytesbury's response was far from comforting. After gathering eyewitness accounts from across Ireland, he wrote, "These reports continue to be of a very alarming nature, and leave no doubt upon the mind but that the potato crops have failed almost everywhere." But he reassured Peel that there was still time to act before food shortages reached a crisis level: "There will be enough saved for immediate consumption. The evil will probably not be felt in all its intensity till towards the month of February, or beginning of spring."[4]

THE SCIENTIFIC COMMISSION

Wanting to know more about the blight and its possible effects, Peel assembled a three-man scientific commission. The commissioners set out for Ireland with instructions to determine exactly what the blight was and to figure out ways to save the portion of the potato crop that was not yet affected. After researching the problem, the commissioners decided that the rotting was not due to a disease, but instead to the unusually cold and wet weather Ireland had recently experienced. They were correct that the weather had made the blight worse. (That year, the blight in the parts of Europe experiencing a drought was far less damaging to the potato harvest.) But the commissioners were completely wrong about the underlying cause of the blight.

Only decades later did scientists learn what the blight was and how it came to Ireland. The blight turned out to be a fungus, spread by spores transported by the wind. The spores could be caught on the underside of leaves of potato plants. A heavy rain could then cause these spores to fall to the ground, where they infected the buried potato tubers.

The blight originated in the Americas. In the early 1840s, it destroyed several seasons of potato crops in the eastern United States. It may have been carried to Europe in cargo ships leaving

A type of potato blight is seen in the flesh damage to this potato. In addition to getting the cause of the blight wrong, the Scientific Commission set up to study the famine gave faulty instructions to farmers about how best to protect their crops from further infestation.

ports such as Philadelphia, Pennsylvania; Baltimore, Maryland; and New York City. It may also have arrived on diseased potatoes shipped with guano imported from South America. Guano was bird excrement that was widely used as fertilizer.

In addition to getting the cause of the blight wrong, the Scientific Commission also issued detailed instructions on how to save healthy potatoes that proved worthless. The commissioners declared that potatoes that did not show signs of the blight should be kept dry and stored in layers in pits covered by a thatch roof to keep the potatoes well ventilated. The government distributed 70,000 copies of their instructions. To their irritation, farmers found that the time-consuming storage methods did little to protect their crop. One newspaper, the *Freeman's Journal*, voiced the popular disgust with the Scientific Commission's advice: "The present commissioners have satisfactorily proved that they know nothing whatever about the causes of or remedies for the disease."[5]

The Scientific Commission made still another faulty claim, but this one actually helped the Irish, who were worried about how they would survive a potato-less spring and summer. The commissioners reported that half of the Irish potato crop had been lost to the blight, adding that they were afraid this appraisal might be too optimistic. In fact, only about one-quarter to one-third of the crop was infected. The commission's over-estimation, however, forced Peel's government to realize it had to take action in order to avoid a horrible humanitarian crisis.

IMPORTING CORN

Prominent Irish citizens urged Prime Minister Peel to stop the exportation of grain from Ireland. They argued that, with famine looming, it was madness to continue to ship food grown in Ireland for sale in England. For Peel to prohibit the Irish exports, however, he would need to repeal what were known as the Corn Laws if the English were to have uninterrupted access to grain. The Corn Laws had established high taxes on most foreign food crops imported to Britain and Ireland and were strongly supported by English merchants and traders. The taxes discouraged foreign countries from selling crops in the United Kingdom. As a result, the price of locally grown food remained high, and traders earned more money.

While Peel supported the repeal of the Corn Laws, other politicians in his party, the Tories, did not. The fight over the Corn Laws ended with Peel being forced from office. But once the opposition party, the Whigs, found they could not put a cabinet together, Peel once again became prime minister.

Because so many government officials were unwilling to support Peel's efforts to help the Irish, he decided to go behind their backs. With his cabinet's approval, he secretly ordered the purchase of £100,000 worth of Indian corn from the United States in early November. Indian corn was a variety of corn that was not traded in Britain, and therefore was largely exempt from regulation by the Corn Laws.

Peel also set up the Relief Commission. This commission, headed by Sir Randolph Routh, was charged with organizing the work of more than 600 local relief groups located throughout Ireland. These relief committees were supposed to set up food depots, where the Indian corn could be sold to people without potatoes. In theory, poor Irish without enough money to buy the corn would be provided rations for free.

Even though the corn shipments started arriving in February 1846, the Relief Commission did not want to distribute food that early. In many places, the potato stores had not yet run out. The commissioners also wanted to encourage the Irish landlords to step up and help the poor living on their estates. If the Indian corn were distributed too soon, they argued, the landlords would not have any reason to take responsibility for their tenants.

The first food depots were opened in late March in the city of Cork. The *Illustrated London News* reported that the poor there were frantic to buy the corn, which was sold at cost—that is, at the same low price at which the government had purchased it: "Immediately on the depots being opened, the crowds of poor persons who gathered round them were so turbulently inclined as to require the immediate interference of the police, who remained there throughout the day."[6]

Depots in other regions were slowly established. Unfortunately, some remote areas did not have access to the government corn until well into May. The amount of corn offered also varied from place to place. Some depots were well supplied; others did not have near enough corn to feed the hungry. Low supplies particularly plagued the south and west, where the need was greatest.

PEEL'S BRIMSTONE

As their potato stores were depleted, the Irish welcomed the government's food relief program. But initially, even the hungry were reluctant to eat Indian corn. It was not nearly as filling as their potato diet had been. Kernels of Indian corn also had a hard shell. If it was not properly ground, it was very hard to digest. When people ate badly ground corn, they often suffered extreme pain in their bowels. The Irish nicknamed the corn "Peel's brimstone,"[7] thereby equating the effects it had on their bodies with the tortures of Hell.

"GREAT MISERY AND WANT"

In May 1846, as food grew scarce throughout Ireland, the *Freeman's Journal* sent a correspondent to County Clare to report on the "State of the South," one of the poorest regions in Ireland. The reporter found a population struggling to survive, with little aid except that provided by religious charities:

> My first visit was to the village of Doonass, about eight miles from Limerick, where I had been informed there was great misery and want. . . . There were about thirty houses here, and not a single potato (if I expect a few remaining rotten ones) with any of the people. They at present subsist on Indian meal purchased in Limerick; but the means of the people are nearly exhausted, and they are in the utmost consternation at the prospect of utter destitution which is staring them full in the face. . . .
>
> At the village of Doonass, I found over 300 families—principally women, young and old—assembled around the petty sessions home, where the Rev. Mr. McMahon, P.P.,

The Relief Commission tried to alleviate the problem by publishing a pamphlet that explained how to cook the corn so as to minimize digestive troubles. It suggested combining the corn with water, milk, or broth to make a thick mush. The pamphlet was very popular with the Irish, although it was useless to the many poor who were illiterate. By the middle of April, the commission's leader, Routh, reported that he "could not have believed that the Indian corn meal would have become so popular."[8]

The corn's popularity should hardly have been so surprising. By the summer, the Irish were desperate for any food they

and one of his assistant curates, with two gentlemen belonging to the neighborhood, were giving out Indian meal to the starving people. It was a melancholy sight, and perhaps one of the most touching I have yet beheld. There were the representatives of at least over 1,000 human beings collected about the place, all eager to get their bags filled with meal, in order to carry it to their famishing children and families. Would that some landlords and legislators had witnessed the scene. The faithful clergy assisting their flocks in the trying hour of need, whilst the landlords, who are morally bound to take care of the persons from whom they derive their incomes, remain in listless apathy, and leave the people to their fate. . . .

I have never witnessed anything like the scene that was presented at Doonass: the creatures crowded around the windows of the house—the doors had to be closed; it was pitiable to hear the implorings of the mothers and daughters beseeching the reverend gentlemen to let them go at once as their children, fathers, or families were waiting at home for food.*

* Noel Kissane, *The Irish Famine: A Documentary History*. Dublin: National Library of Ireland, 1995, p. 40.

THE PICTORIAL TIMES.

A SCENE IN TARMONS. — A WIDOW AND CHILDREN OF THE O'CONNELL ESTATES ON THEIR WAY TO BEG POTATOES.

In this 1846 illustration, a widow and her children go off to beg for food. Some Irish were so starved that they begged admittance into British workhouses.

could get their hands on. Charities run by Quakers—members of the religious group now known as the Religious Society of Friends—noted that the demand for aid was far outstripping supply. One Quaker report claimed that the poorest were now clamoring for admittance into the hated workhouses, a fate most of them would have considered unthinkable just months before. The report described

poor wretches in the last stage of famine imploring to be received into the house; women who had six or seven children begging that even two or three of them might be taken in. . . . Some of these children were worn to skeletons, their features sharpened with hunger, and their limbs wasted almost to the bone.[9]

LOOKING FORWARD

Even so, Peel's purchase of Indian corn was a qualified success. The food might not have been evenly distributed or offered in a timely manner, but few Irish died of starvation because of the blight in late 1845 and early 1846. Although prices rose as food became scarce, by selling imported Indian corn at cost, Peel was at least able to keep prices from escalating sky-high.

Modern historians generally praise Peel for his actions during the early period of the Great Irish Famine. But in his day, his fellow politicians criticized him for his efforts. In June 1846, he finally succeeded in eliminating the import taxes on food—a stance so unpopular with his own party members that they ousted him from power. Lord John Russell, leader of the rival Whig Party, replaced him as prime minister.

Unlike Peel, who had been in Ireland during an earlier famine, Russell did not have any real familiarity with the Irish. An aristocratic son of a duke, he in fact had little contact with any poor people. Still, few worried about how Russell would handle another food shortage in Ireland. Although occasional famines were not unknown there, they always lasted just a single growing season. Having just suffered and survived the latest crop failure, the Irish looked forward to a healthy potato harvest that would once again turn such desperate times into a memory.

The Crisis Grows

During the summer of 1846, William Steuart Trench, a land agent and speculator with farm properties in Ireland, frequently traveled to the countryside to see what he later called his "splendid mountain crop." After the disastrous harvest the previous year, he was thrilled to see the potato plants on his lands growing to "a healthy and abundant maturity." But during one visit, his excitement over his prosperous future was totally squelched:

On August 6, 1846—I shall not readily forget the day—I rode up as usual to my mountain property. . . . I could scarcely bear the fearful and strange smell, which came up so rank from the luxuriant crop then growing all around; no perceptible change, except the smell, had as yet come upon the apparent prosperity of the deceitfully luxuriant stalks, but the experience of the past few days taught me that all was gone, and the crop was utterly worthless.[1]

Trench desperately dug up his potato plants, hoping against all evidence that he could salvage at least part of the crop. But the devastation was complete. As he later wrote, "My plans, my labour, my £3,000, and all hopes of future profit by these means were gone!"[2]

For Trench, the blight's return meant that he had lost a fortune. For most people in Ireland, however, this grim discovery was far more threatening. Instead of worrying about loss of income, they were terrified that they might lose their lives. How could the Irish people possible survive another year without a healthy potato crop?

The bad news only grew worse. This time, the blight had struck earlier in the growing season and had a far more devastating effect. Only about one-quarter of the crop could be saved. Adding to the catastrophe, the number of acres planted in 1846 had dropped by more than 20 percent of those planted in 1845 because farmers had had a shortage of seed potatoes. As a result, the total potato crop could keep the Irish fed for only one month. The situation was so terrible that the Irish could scarcely believe it. As a Quaker report recounted, "The announcement of this dreadful calamity did not at first produce the alarm which might have been expected. The idea of millions being reduced to starvation was too great to be quickly realised."[3]

CHANGING RELIEF POLICIES

Just as people began to understand the scope of the disaster, the relief programs set up under Prime Minister Peel were being dismantled. The new government headed by Lord John Russell was shutting down Ireland's food depots. It also began laying off workers hired by a modest jobs program Peel had established.

Because of their political beliefs, Russell and his Whig Party opposed any government aid to the poor, apart from the workhouse system its government had created with the Poor Law Amendment Act of 1834. They thought it would hurt the economy if the government sold or gave away food. In general, they considered it a mistake for the government to interfere with any economic markets, though the party had done so previously when it outlawed slavery in the British Empire with the Slavery Abolition Act of 1833. That said, most Whigs at the time believed that merchants and traders alone should be able to set the price for the food they sold, without government interference.

Aside from their economic argument for denying aid, the Whigs also felt that government relief posed a moral problem. They subscribed to the common belief of the day that the poor were poor because they did not work hard enough. They felt this was especially true of the Irish poor. Many English people harbored deep prejudices against the Irish. Their contempt was partly based on religion: English Protestants tended to look down on Irish Catholics as social and moral inferiors. If the Irish received aid, some argued, these lazy people would never learn the value of hard work and self-sufficiency.

TREVELYAN AND THE IRISH

Such anti-Irish views were strongly held by Charles Trevelyan, the assistant secretary of the British Treasury who was charged with implementing the Irish relief policies of the Russell government. Trevelyan despised not only the Irish poor but also the Irish landlords. He held them largely responsible for the famine because they had overseen an economic system that had become overly reliant on the yearly potato crop. He later wrote:

> A population, whose ordinary food is wheat and beef, and whose ordinary drink is porter and ale, can retrench in periods of scarcity, and resort to cheaper kinds of food, such as barley, oats, rice, and potatoes. But those who are habitually and entirely fed on potatoes live upon the extreme verge of human subsistence, and when they are deprived of their

Sir Charles Edward Trevelyan was the one British civil servant most infamously connected with the Irish famine. As assistant treasury secretary, he administered the British government's meager response to the famine. His personal animosity toward the Irish is today seen as helping to worsen the crisis.

accustomed food, there is nothing cheaper to which they can resort. They have already reached the lowest point in the descending scale, and there is nothing beyond but starvation or beggary.[4]

CHARLES TREVELYAN

Charles Trevelyan is one of the most controversial figures in Irish history. Born on April 2, 1807, Trevelyan was the son of a Protestant clergyman. At 19, he began his long career in civil service. Trevelyan moved to India, which was then part of the British Empire. In Delhi, he worked to better the living conditions of Indians and modernize their trade practices. Later, in Calcutta, Trevelyan helped establish schools for the local population.

Two years after returning to England in 1838, Trevelyan was named the assistant secretary to the Treasury. He held this post for 19 years, during which he oversaw the British government's efforts to provide relief to Irish famine victims. Like John Russell, the second prime minister under whom he served, Trevelyan sought to intervene in the crisis as little as possible. He strongly opposed distribution of food, because it would disrupt the business of food merchants and traders and because it would make the Irish poor too dependent on the government. Trevelyan also refused to consider banning the export of grain from Ireland, a position that led to rioting by irate Irish.

Most historians now contend that Trevelyan's cold and unyielding views about famine relief were in large part responsible for making the disaster far worse than it should have been. Some maintain that his anti-Catholic views

Trevelyan also believed that the crop failure was an act of God intended to punish the Irish. In his eyes, therefore, the impending famine could be considered a blessing. As the Irish population dropped, Ireland would become less dependent on

helped make him unmoved by news of the suffering and dying Irish. Certainly, in his own writings about the famine, Trevelyan left little doubt that he held the Irish in contempt: "The judgement of God sent the calamity to teach the Irish a lesson, that calamity must not be too much mitigated. . . . The real evil with which we have to contend is not the physical evil of the Famine, but the moral evil of the selfish, perverse and turbulent character of the people."*

His bold denunciation of an entire people is repellent today, but in his time, Trevelyan's beliefs were lauded by many English elites, especially in the government. In 1848, Queen Victoria even knighted Trevelyan for his administration of famine relief.

Trevelyan was also well regarded in England for his efforts to reform the civil service. Working with Sir Stafford Northcote, he issued a report, suggesting educational requirements for civil servants and competitive exams for job applicants. After leaving the Treasury, Trevelyan returned to India, where he served as the finance minister from 1862 to 1865. He spent the remainder of his life in England working for a variety of charities. Trevelyan died in London on June 19, 1886. Since then, many histories of the famine have represented him as a villain who was either wholly or partly responsible for the unnecessary mass death of the era.

---

* "Charles Edward Trevelyan." Multitext Project in Irish History, University College Cork, Ireland. http://multitext.ucc.ie/d/ Charles_Edward_Trevelyan.

the potato. It would also compel the Irish landlords and other elite to learn to take better care of their economy and society.

Trevelyan's cruel worldview greatly influenced Russell's plans for Irish aid, which the prime minister outlined in a speech to the British Parliament's House of Commons on August 17, 1846. Russell vowed that the government would no longer "interfere with the regular mode by which Indian corn and other kinds of grain may be brought into the country."[5] Food depots would be confined to western Ireland only. Further buckling to the demand of food merchants, he declared that they alone would determine the price of all food sold.

With mass starvation looming, however, Russell felt he had to offer some aid to the Irish poor. But he still held that giving them food would be morally wrong, because it would make the poor even more dependent and lazy. Instead, the government would set up a large public works program that would hire unemployed and destitute breadwinners. Such a program would, he believed, provide relief from the worst suffering and instill the value of hard work that he and his peers believed was so lacking in the Irish.

RISING PRICES AND EXPORTS

Many Irish landowners were happy with Russell's relief works program. Because the government provided loans for the capital needed to get the public works up and running, the program gave the landlords a cheap way of making improvements to their property. Proposals for projects from landlords flooded into the Board of Works, which was to administer the relief works. Charged with reviewing possible projects and getting them going, the board grew into a massive, disorganized bureaucracy, eventually employing 12,000 people. The inefficiency of the Board of Works made it impossible to get the relief works operating quickly.

In the meantime, the Irish were growing desperate as their meager potato stores dwindled. Few could find employment, so they were unable to buy food. Even those who earned a wage could often not afford to purchase food at the market rates. In the final months of 1846, shortages had caused food prices to skyrocket. For instance, from September to November, the price of a ton of Indian corn meal rose from £11 to £18. Russell's efforts to allow traders and merchants to set prices was paying off handsomely while most of the population was facing starvation.

Even though the potato supply was nearly exhausted, Russell's government continued to allow Irish grain to be exported. Routh wrote to Trevelyan, urging him to end the exports: "I know there is a great and serious objection to any interference with these exports, yet it is a most serious evil."[6] Trevelyan, however, still refused to change his policies.

The Irish public became irate at the sight of ships full of grain leaving Irish ports. Several riots broke out, most notably at Dungarvan in County Waterford. On October 3, 1846, the *Waterford Freeman* reported on the incident: "The women assembled in Dungarvan on Thursday, and prevented the loading of the vessel with grain. They did this in the presence of the military, and in defiance of the civil authorities. Do not such acts speak volumes to the government?"[7] During the melee, police fired into the crowd, killing one rioter and injuring several more.

THE RELIEF WORKS PROGRAM

After long delays, the relief works program started to provide employment to some of the needy. The Board of Works could have selected a variety of projects that would boost the Irish economy in the long term. For instance, constructing piers and harbors could have modernized the fishing industry in coastal areas. But instead, nearly all the projects the board approved involved building or improving roads. Road building projects were relatively easy to organize, but many of them had no real practical use. Some in remote areas literally produced roads to nowhere.

In this 1846 illustration taken from the *Pictorial Times*, a crowd attempts to break into a bakery during the food riots in Dungarvan, County Waterford.

The relief works were rife with corruption. Local relief committees determined who got hired. In order to work, a laborer had to present an official ticket provided by a committee. The jobs were supposed to go to "persons who are destitute of means of support, or for whose support such employment is actually necessary."[8] But often committee members overlooked the destitute to give the jobs to their friends. In some cases, corrupt committees simply sold tickets to the highest bidder.

Moreover, relief jobs were sometimes unavailable in the regions that needed them most. In extremely poor areas, people were often scattered across the countryside. They were not unified enough to have leaders who might be able to persuade the government to create a relief works project in the region.

Even if a remote area had relief jobs, the pay due to workers was often delayed. Before the famine, the Irish poor generally traded goods with one another. In many places, money was very rarely used. Just getting currency to pay workers in these areas proved a challenge. In other cases, mistakes in paperwork prevented workers from getting paid on time. In October 1846, a worker named Denis McKennedy keeled over and died in the town of Skibbereen. The coroner's office discovered that the pay the government owed him was two weeks late. It found that he had "died of starvation due to the gross negligence of the Board of Works."[9]

Workers awaiting pay could sometimes buy food on credit. But merchants who extended credit charged exorbitant prices. Even with pay in hand, some laborers faced enormous obstacles in buying food. According to William Edward Forster, an English Quaker involved in the relief efforts, "Often the poor people have, after earning their wretched pittance at the public works, to walk ten, twenty, even thirty miles to the nearest store to get a stone of meal."[10]

WORKING HARD FOR LITTLE PAY

Another problem relief workers faced was low wages. As food prices rose, the money they received could buy less and less. By November 1846, a man with a relief job earned about 8 shillings a week. But by then it cost about 21 shillings a week to feed an average family.

The government made matters worse when it started paying workers by the task rather than by the day. English officials,

fixated on the supposed laziness of the Irish, feared that laborers would work too slowly if they were guaranteed a certain
amount of pay each day. (In fact, Irish workers did sometimes
draw out their work, both to conserve their energy and to
prevent the loss of their job once the road they were working
on was completed.) By instituting pay by task, the government
ensured that laborers who performed the most work would be
paid the most.

The Irish hated the task-work system. For almost all of the
workers, it resulted in a sizable drop in income. It also favored
the young and healthy over the old and ill. Some work crews
tried to ban such less-productive workers because they would
drag down the pay of everyone else. Defining tasks and measuring the work done by each worker was also a daunting chore
for local relief committees to take on. Workers sometimes
threatened officials who they felt were cheating them out of pay
by incorrectly measuring the amount of work they performed.

Relief work jobs required workers to perform hard physical labor for some 10 hours a day. As food grew scarce, even
once-strong men became too malnourished to work that long.
Many workers also had to walk many miles from their houses
to their jobs each day. By the time they arrived to work, they
were sometimes too weak to stand. Adding to their misery, the
winter of 1846–1847 was unusually cold and wet, forcing starving workers to spend many hours outside exposed to punishing
winds, rain, and snow.

Long after the famine, the Irish remembered the relief
works program with enormous bitterness. Many could not help
but see it as a plot concocted by the British government to force
the Irish to suffer as much as possible. Sixty years later, Hugh
Dorian published a history of the brutal winter of 1846–1847
based on the accounts of those who had lived through it. He
condemned the government "for slowly taking away human
life, getting rid of the population and nothing else, by forcing
the hungry and the half-dead men to stand out in the cold and

in the sleet and rain from morn till night for the paltry reward of nine pennies per day." Dorian concluded that if British officials had offered the dying Irish a meager allowance without forcing them to leave their homes "it would convey the impression that their benefactors meant to save life, but in the way [the relief was] thus given, on compulsory conditions, meant next to slow murder."[11]

5

Starvation
and Disease

As 1847 began, conditions in Ireland were worse than ever. The previous winter, when the stores of potatoes were empty, the poor still had access to low-cost and sometimes free Indian corn. This year, however, the inadequacies and cruelties of the government's relief program left many without any food at all. Unable to endure the winds and snows of a brutal winter, people began to die of starvation. They were said to have dropsy, the then-popular term for hunger edema. Prior to death, the bodies and limbs of edema victims swelled grotesquely as water accumulated in their bodily cavities or tissues.

But during this horrific period, many more people succumbed to another scourge—infectious disease. Then as now, disease often accompanies famine. When people are malnourished, they lose much of their resistance to infection. In addition, when they do become sick, they are much more likely to die. Populations severely weakened by food shortages are also unable to be as attentive to proper sanitation and personal hygiene, which can encourage the spread of epidemic disease.

FAMINE FEVER

In 1847, the starving Irish were vulnerable to a variety of diseases. One of the most common was bacillus dysentery, popularly known as the bloody flux. Spread through flies and contaminated food and water, dysentery caused extreme diarrhea and was very painful. Many people also suffered from diarrhea and other intestinal problems because, in their struggle to survive, they tried eating grasses and bark, which humans cannot easily digest.

Other common diseases included ophthalmia, an eye infection that could lead to blindness, and scurvy, which caused a sufferer's teeth to fall out. A lack of vitamin C in the diet leads to scurvy. Previously, it had been virtually unknown in Ireland, because the potato was so nutritious. Some diseases proved particularly deadly to young people. The lung disease tuberculosis struck many teenagers, while measles was particularly menacing to young children. When a village was felled with an epidemic of measles, all of its children could be dead within a matter of days.

Perhaps most dreaded of all was famine fever. The term was used to describe two different diseases—typhus and relapsing fever—that are caused by microorganisms carried on lice, which live on the skin and clothing. Typhus, sometimes called black fever, affected the circulation of the blood and gave a sufferer a blotchy rash and darkened skin. The relapsing fever was known as yellow fever. Attacking the stomach and liver, it could lead to jaundice, a condition that caused the skin to yellow.

In the early months of 1847, much of Ireland was overrun with famine fever. It was especially widespread in the south and west, regions that had the highest concentration of people, as well as the largest number of the poor. Famine fever, however, was not only a rural phenomenon. Starving farm workers who flooded into towns and cities unknowingly carried such deadly diseases into these urban centers. Because their population density helped spread sickness, many cities experienced severe epidemics. In Dublin and Belfast, streets were littered with the dead and dying. Each morning, shopkeepers came upon the corpses of people who had spent the night huddling for warmth in the stores' doorways.

People sick with fever also flocked to cities because they were home to the few medical facilities in Ireland. At the beginning of the typhus epidemic, all of Ireland had only 28 hospitals, most of which were in urban centers. A noted physician named William Wilde, the father of the famous Irish playwright Oscar Wilde, later described the strain the epidemic had placed on the hospitals in cities such as Dublin, Cork, and Waterford: "There, day after day, numbers of people, wasted by famine and consumed by fever, could be seen lying on the footpaths and roads waiting for the chance of admission; and when they were fortunate enough to be received, their places were soon filled by other victims of suffering and disease."[1]

DISEASE IN THE WORKHOUSE

The British government's famine policies also made the epidemics worse. By forcing people to leave their scattered homes and congregate at food depots and relief work projects, they brought sick people in close contact with the healthy, causing them to become ill as well. This problem was especially acute in the workhouses.

The workhouse system in Ireland was originally designed to accommodate about 100,000 people. Before the famine, the workhouses were so reviled that usually no more than 38,000 people were in the system at any one time. As the food shortages worsened in 1847, however, more and more starving Irish

By 1846, the famine had grown so bad that starving peasants clamored to get through the gates of British workhouses, institutions so hated by the Irish that they were shunned in better times.

flooded into workhouses. As one government report noted, "a supply of food, even of tolerable quality and in moderate quantity, yet provided regularly and without fail, becomes almost irresistibly attractive to the poor."[2] Officials did whatever they could to keep poor out. They provided no heat in the winter and reduced the food rations offered. Even so, conditions were so desperate that many begged for admission. Parents were particularly insistent in trying to get their sons and daughters taken in. As horrible as the workhouses were, these parents believed that living there would give their children their only chance for survival.

As the workhouses became overcrowded, they turned into death traps. With people living in close quarters, infectious diseases swept through the facilities, causing death at a horrifying rate. By April 1847, 25 out of every 1,000 residents perished every week in the workhouses.

The problem was exacerbated as the Irish's funerary traditions broke down. Funerals and wakes had once been an important part of Irish life. Even the poorest families managed

"THE DEATHS ... WERE MANY AND HORRIBLE"

To commemorate the one hundredth anniversary of the Great Irish Famine, the Irish Folklore Commission circulated questionnaires to the descendants of the survivors, asking them to recount the direct memories of the era their relatives had shared with them. Many of these memories, such as those excerpted below, dealt with the hasty burial of the dead during the famine years. Traditionally, the Irish had taken their elaborate funerary rituals very seriously. As a result, being unable to provide their dead friends and relatives a proper burial remained a source of sorrow and guilt for many years after the disaster.

From Croom, County Limerick:
The deaths in my native place were many and horrible. The poor famine-stricken people were found by the wayside, emaciated corpses, partly green from eating docks and nettles, and partly blue from the cholera and dysentery. They were buried where they were found. . . . The ditch [raised fence] was then built over the body and some stones set into the breastwork of the fence to mark

to provide their deceased relatives with spirited sendoffs to the afterlife. But as the death toll rose, there were often not enough family members alive to bury the dead, much less give them a proper funeral. Instead of placing the dead in coffins and taking them to graveyards, corpses were unceremoniously dumped into sacks and buried in the grounds near their houses.

Although no one at the time knew what caused the diseases that were decimating the population, the Irish poor realized

the grave. . . . I know two places pointed out to me by my mother nearly half a century ago where such burials took place.

From Boherbue, County Cork:
South of Boherbue there is a famous Famine graveyard at Sceac [Scagh]. . . . About forty years ago an Australian called to see the place. He was fairly old and said his father, an emigrant, often worked conveying the Famine victims to Scagh graveyard. His father had the large box and it was used again and again carrying the corpses. They were often buried together in one hole. Scagh graveyard has not been used since the Famine days and is very neglected.

From Coalisland, County Tyrone:
Deaths occurred from disease rather than from starvation, and owing to the long distance to the graveyard and the weakness of the survivors, it is known that some were buried in fields near the dwellings. Such burial places were marked by a tree. . . . Where there were several deaths in one house, the bodies were rolled into sacking and buried without coffin of any kind.*

* Noel Kissane, *The Irish Famine: A Documentary History.* Dublin: National Library of Ireland, 1995, p. 120.

that handling a dead body could put them at risk for infection. Therefore, people who were dying of diseases feared that their corpses would never be buried, but instead just be left outside to rot. As a result, in their last days, some people went to the workhouse hoping that the government would see to it that they received coffins and decent burials. The large number of dying made it all the more difficult for other workhouse residents to remain disease-free.

Workhouses were ill equipped to deal with the mounting dead. Officials were forced to begin loading their bodies into reusable coffins with hinged bottoms. Opening the hinge, they dumped each corpse into a mass grave dug outside the workhouse. One eyewitness described how residents near death were taken to the "black room" at the workhouse in the town of Castlerea: "From the window in this room there were a few boards slanting down to the earth, and beneath was a huge grave or pit. When a death occurred, the corpse was allowed to slide down the boards into the pit beneath, and lime was put over the corpse."[3]

THE IRISH FEVER ACT

Although the typhus epidemic of 1847 took a terrible toll on the Irish poor, it was ironically an even greater threat to wealthier urban people. Many of the poor in the countryside had previously had some exposure to typhus, so they had developed at least some natural immunity to the disease. The more well-to-do, however, generally had no immunities and therefore were far more likely to die of typhus if they were infected. The poor-law commissioners used the vulnerability of the wealthier Irish to scare government officials into dealing with the epidemic. They wrote in a report:

> Although fever may commence its ravages amongst the poorer classes, it scarcely ever fails, ultimately, to visit the rich; and it is to be observed that the mortality amongst rich

persons affected with fever in Ireland is nearly ten times as great as amongst the poor under similar circumstances. . . . Hence, expenses incurred for the cure of destitute fever patients may be regarded to a certain extent as a kind of life insurance to the rich who are in health.[4]

The British Parliament responded to the crisis by passing the Irish Fever Act in April 1847. Through the Central Board of Health, it allowed for the creation of about 100 temporary fever hospitals. Workhouses were also encouraged to establish wooden fever sheds, where the sick could be isolated from the healthy. Many workhouses, however, were so bankrupt that they did not have enough money to create these separate facilities.

Between July 1847 and August 1850, about 580,000 people were treated in the fever hospitals. But that statistic grossly underestimates the number of people affected by epidemic disease. The vast majority of the diseases' victims were never admitted to any medical facilities. No exact death toll has ever been recorded, because deaths were left unregistered during the famine years. Some experts hold that for every victim of starvation, there were 10 more who died from the many diseases that ravaged Ireland during this era.

Feeding the Hungry

After the second failure of Ireland's potato crop, British newspapers published many reports about the starving Irish. When these accounts first appeared, the English public was highly sympathetic to the suffering of their countrymen. Many people contributed to charities that had been formed to help provide food and aid to Ireland.

Among the most effective was the British Association for the Relief of the Extreme Distress in Ireland and Scotland, which was established on January 1, 1847. The organization approached prominent figures and businesses for donations. Despite their personal feelings toward the Irish, Prime Minister Russell and Assistant Treasury Secretary Trevelyan both gave large contributions. Supposedly when Queen Victoria, the British monarch, was asked to contribute, she at first offered

£1,000. Disappointed by the amount, the organization shamed her into doubling her donation. (Among the Irish poor, a rumor spread that Queen Victoria had given the charity a mere £5.) In total, the British Association raised more than £470,000 for famine relief.

Accounts of the famine were also widely reported in other parts of the world. Charitable donations flooded in from many countries, including India, South Africa, Italy, and Jamaica. The American Indians of the Choctaw Nation were among those offering help. Their recent history made them sympathetic to the plight of the Irish. Less than a decade earlier, they had been forced by the U.S. government to move from their homeland in the Southeast to Indian Territory (now Oklahoma). During their brutal trek west, many Choctaws suffered from hunger and died of disease.

Americans and Canadians were particularly generous in raising money for Ireland. Long before the famine began, there had been a steady stream of Irish immigrants into these countries. Most were young men who saw immigration as their best means for building a better life. Although some Irish immigrants were attracted to North America by the lure of inexpensive or free land, most settled in cities, where they generally lived in slum neighborhoods filled with other Irish immigrants. There, they worked hard to raise funds to help feed their starving friends and relatives back home.

CHARITY FROM THE QUAKERS

The Quakers, who had a long history in philanthropic work, provided some of the most effective famine relief. In the second year of the famine, Quaker leaders formed the Central Relief Committee of the Society of Friends. The committee decided that the Quakers' strategy for combating the famine would focus on setting up soup kitchens, where the hungry would be given food at a very low price. The Quakers carefully planned a recipe for a nutritious soup, which included beef, peas, oatmeal, and barley. In a report, the committee members conceded that "a very palatable soup could be made at a much lower cost,"[1] but they argued that, if they were to have any success in elimi-

"INDEED THE HUNGER"

In March 1847, an English Quaker named William Bennett traveled to County Mayo to provide an eyewitness account of the famine to his church's officials. The following is an excerpt from his report:

The scenes of human misery and degradation we wit-nessed still haunt my imagination with the vividness and power of some horrid and tyrannous delusion rather than the features of a sober reality. We entered a cabin. Stretched in one dark corner . . . were three children huddled together, lying there because they were too weak to rise, pale and ghastly; their little limbs, on removing a portion of the filthy covering, perfectly emaciated, eyes sunk, voice gone, and evidently in the last stage of actual starvation. Crouched over the turf embers was another form, wild and all but naked, scarcely human in appearance. It stirred not, nor noticed us. On some straw, soddened upon the ground, moaning piteously, was a shrivelled old woman, implor-ing us to give her something, baring her limbs partly, to show how the skin hung loose from the bones. . . . Above her, on something like a ledge, was a young woman, with sunken cheeks, a mother, I have no doubt, who scarcely raised her eyes in answer to our enquiries, but pressed her hand upon her forehead, with a look of unutterable anguish and despair.

nating malnutrition and epidemic disease, the soup they gave to the poor had to be rich in nutrients.

In November 1846, the Quakers set up their first soup kitchen in Cork. With donated soup boilers, they established

Many cases were widows whose husbands had recently been taken off by the fever, and thus their only pittance, obtained from the public works, was entirely cut off. In many, the husbands or sons were prostate under that horrid disease, the results of long-continued famine and low living, in which first the limbs, and then the body, swell most frightfully and finally burst. We entered upwards of fifty of these tenements. The scene was invariably the same. . . . The whole number was often not to be distinguished, until, the eye having adapted itself to the darkness, they were pointed out, or were heard, or some filthy bundle of rags and straw was perceived to move.

Perhaps the poor children presented the most piteous and heart-rending spectacle. Many were too weak to stand, their little limbs attenuated, except where the frightful swellings had taken the place of previous emaciation. Every infantile expression had entirely departed; and, in some, reason and intelligence had evidently flown. Many were remnants of families, crowded together in one cabin, orphaned little relatives, taken in by the equally destitute, and even strangers; for these poor people are kind to one another to the end. In one cabin was a sister, just dying, lying by the side of her little brother, just dead. I have worse than this to relate, but it is useless to multiply details, and they are in fact unfit. They did but rarely complain. When we enquired what was the matter, the answer was alike in all: "Tha shein ukrosh," "indeed the hunger."*

* Noel Kissane, *The Irish Famine: A Documentary History.* Dublin: National Library of Ireland, 1995, p. 117.

Seen here in this 1847 illustration, a soup house set up by Quakers in Cork to provide relief for those affected by the failure of the potato harvest. The charity work done by the Quakers was among the most effective forms of relief during the Irish famine.

hundreds more. Each kitchen could produce as much as 1,500 gallons of soup a day at a cost of between £120 and £150 a month. The Quaker soup kitchens saved the lives of many Irish people, especially during the spring of 1847 when the government's relief efforts were falling far short of what was needed.

Other charities also found serving soup as an economical way of helping the starving. In some cases, landlords established their own soup kitchens for the tenants on their estates. As Irish activist and journalist John Mitchel later wrote:

> Irish landlords . . . are not all monsters of cruelty. . . . [T]he resident landlords and their families did, in many cases, devote themselves to the task of saving their poor people alive. Many remitted their rents, or half their rents; and ladies kept their servants busy and their kitchens smoking with continual preparation of food for the poor.[2]

A NEW STRATEGY

By early 1847, the British government's primary mechanism for providing aid to the Irish—the relief works program—was in complete disarray. The Board of Works could not keep up with the demand for jobs from the desperate and the poor. By March 1847, about 714,000 people had relief jobs. Most were men who supported their families with their meager wages. Probably a total of at least 3 million people depended on income from government jobs for their livelihood. Employing so many people came at a high cost. The government was spending almost £1 million a month on relief works.

At the same time, the workhouse system was unraveling. By February 1847, about 116,000 Irish people lived in workhouses, including about 63,000 children. Already overcrowded, the workhouses were besieged every day with crowds of starving men, women, and children begging to be allowed inside. The costs of running the workhouses began to soar at the same time that collecting the taxes that financed them from impoverished landowners was becoming virtually impossible.

An officer of the Board of Works wrote to Charles Trevelyan, urging him to create a new policy toward Irish relief. He encouraged Trevelyan to disband the relief works program: "The fact is that the system . . . is no longer beneficial employment to many; their bodily strength being gone, and spirits depressed, they have not power to exert themselves sufficiently to earn the ordinary day's wages." Impressed by the Quakers' work, the officer suggested that the government adopt a similar approach: "You will perceive the great benefits derived from the soup establishments and how very cheap is the preparation."[3]

The idea went completely against Trevelyan's political philosophy. He thought the government should not interfere with the economy in any way. If the government provided cheap food for the poor, he believed, it would drive food prices down, which would certainly hurt the income of food merchants and traders. He also thought that giving direct aid to the poor was morally wrong, because it would encourage what he saw as their natural tendency toward laziness.

Even more important to Trevelyan, however, was keeping the costs of government low. Although it meant admitting the relief works program had been a total failure, in the end he promoted the idea of establishing soup kitchens because they would be much less expensive to run. With his support, Parliament passed the Act for the Temporary Relief of Destitute Persons in Ireland in February 1847. The new law called for the creation of soup kitchens as a temporary measure. The kitchens were to be dismantled in September, just as the next potato crop was being harvested.

ESTABLISHING SOUP KITCHENS

In April, the government set up a model soup kitchen in Dublin, designed by Alexis Soyer, a well-known French chef. He developed a soup recipe that would be used throughout Ireland. The soup was far less nutritious than the one offered by the Quakers, but it was also considerably cheaper to make.

The government had planned to get about 2,000 soup kitchens up and running. Distribution of soup was supposed to start on March 15, but two months later only 1,250 kitchens were in operation. The government had underestimated how long it would take to establish the new relief effort. Just printing

This illustration shows a soup kitchen exhibited in Dublin by Alexis Soyer. A celebrated Parisian chef, Soyer came to England in 1831, gaining popularity by working for a number of aristocrats before finding fame as chef of the Reform Club. Today, Soyer's philanthropic work is remembered for providing soup kitchens to the Irish during the famine and for improving nutrition for British and French soldiers during the Crimean War (1853–1856).

the 3 million tickets the poor were supposed to present to the kitchens each day proved a hugely daunting task.

As the government struggled to set up the soup kitchens, it began laying people off from the relief works. By June, virtually all workers had been fired. With the delays in the kitchen program, about 15 percent of these newly unemployed workers did not yet have access to the government-subsidized soup. For many families, this bureaucratic mix-up caused extreme deprivation and suffering.

Initially, many Irish disliked the idea of the soup kitchens. With his low opinion of the Irish poor, Trevelyan assumed they would love a government handout, while in fact many felt ashamed when accepting the charity they could no longer afford to refuse. Quickly, though, they embraced the program, which proved not only cheaper than the relief works but also more efficient and humane.

SOUP FOR THE STARVING

Local relief commissions drew up lists of the people in their areas who would qualify to get soup for free. Those earning small wages were allowed to buy soup at a low price. Each day, soup recipients were supposed to line up at their local kitchen with their soup pots in hand. When they reached the front of the line, they presented their ticket. It was printed with a calendar. Before filling a person's pot with his or her ration, a soup kitchen worker would punch a hole in the day's date so that no one else could use the ticket again that day.

Many had to walk miles just to reach their local soup kitchens. They then had to wait in long lines for their share. It was not unusual for starving and sick people to collapse or even die in line. To many proud Irish, the entire ritual was humiliating. In the eyes of government officials, though, that was a positive thing. By making the soup kitchen experience as demoralizing as possible, they believed only the truly destitute would be willing to subject themselves to it. In that way, it kept the number of people receiving aid lower than if the soup were distributed in a less demeaning manner.

Taking pity on those they served, local relief committees sometimes ignored the strict rules set out by the government. For instance, every able-bodied person in a family was supposed to stand in line each day. But at some soup kitchens, the workers gave one family member the soup rations for the rest.

In another example, soup kitchens were instructed to serve only cooked food. Government officials feared that if people received uncooked ingredients, they might try to sell them. They were especially convinced that Irish men would sell their family's only means of sustenance for alcohol or tobacco. Relief workers, though, sometimes offered uncooked food because doing so was cheaper. Many people on the soup line also preferred it, because for those who traveled great distances, the cooked soup might spoil before they could get it home.

The soup kitchen program had many problems. The government was slow about setting it up. The soup offered was often a watery gruel that, if not properly prepared, caused stomach pain and diarrhea. In some kitchens, the soup did not have enough vegetables to ward off scurvy. In others, local relief committees were so pressed for income that they served portions much smaller than those mandated by the government.

But with all these problems, the soup kitchens were the best relief program established by the British government during the entire famine. At a relatively low cost, the kitchens fed about 3 million people a day at the program's height. As the members of one relief committee reported soon after establishing a soup kitchen, "had they not witnessed it themselves, they could scarcely have conceived it possible that such a change for the better could have been brought about in the health and appearance of the poor in so short a time and at comparatively so small an expense."[4]

Leaving Ireland

L ong before the blight struck Ireland, many Irish had chosen to leave their homeland and begin new lives in dis-
tant lands. Between 1815 and 1845, about 1.5 million people
emigrated from Ireland. Most eventually settled in England,
the United States, Canada, and Australia. Because of the cost
of travel, these early immigrants were not usually poor. They
were also generally healthy young men who, while working as
farmers or tradesmen, had amassed enough savings to make
emigration possible.

The pattern of emigration began to change as soon as the
first blackened, rotting tubers were pulled from the ground.
Both 1845 and 1846 saw an uptick of emigration as the failure
of the potato crop convinced many that their best means of
surviving food shortages and disease epidemics was to leave

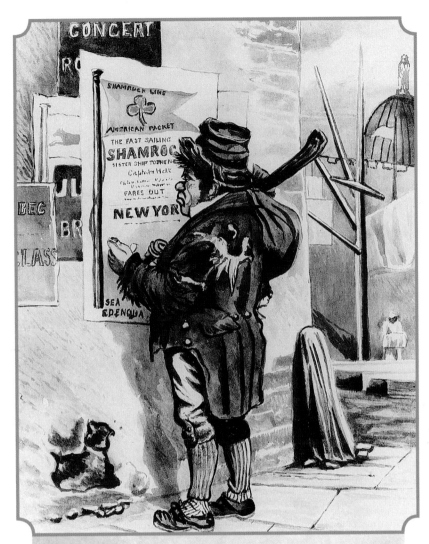

This nineteenth-century cartoon shows an Irishman contemplating immigration to America. The mass exodus of Irish to America starting during the potato famine helped to reshape the makeup of both nations.

Ireland altogether. This rise in the emigration rate turned into an explosion in 1847. By the spring, tens of thousands, having seen the horrors created by two years of famine, were clamoring to escape. In 1847 alone, 250,000 people emigrated from Ireland. For each of the next five years, about 200,000 more would leave annually.

The composition of the emigrants also changed. The vast majority were no longer healthy young men but destitute laborers and their families. Many were sick. Most were malnourished. Driven by desperation, very few had a workable plan for where to go and how to get there.

FUNDING THE TRIP

A small minority of the emigrants had their travels paid by their landlords. While some landlords might have been solely motivated by a desire to save their tenants' lives, most who adopted such as scheme did so as a cost-saving measure.

One example was the Marquis of Lansdowne, whose large estate in County Kerry was home to thousands of tenants. The marquis's agent, William Steuart Trench, wrote his employer to explain that the marquis would be required to pay £15,000 a year to fund famine relief efforts, but in the depressed Irish economy, the estate was taking in only £10,000 annually. Trench concluded that it would be far more economical for the marquis to simply pay for his tenants' emigration than to provide relief. Lansdowne eventually spent only £17,000 to send more than 4,600 people to the United States and Canada. As Trench emphasized, surely many of Lansdowne's tenants were happy to emigrate. But just as surely, at least a few felt that they were being expelled from their homeland against their will.

Lansdowne's tenants were exceptions among the emigrants during the famine years; only about 50,000 received financial assistance from their landlords. A few more were sponsored by charities. But almost all of the emigrants had to find a way to fund their own travel. For instance, farmers might raise the money by selling their remaining livestock or any grain they had left. Workers might receive enough cash from relatives who had emigrated years earlier.

The poorest of would-be emigrants set out without adequate funds at hand. Most headed toward the English port of Liverpool, where ships regularly sailed for the United States and Canada. In Liverpool, they hoped to raise their fares by begging in the streets. The flood of Irish refugees soon overwhelmed the city. By June 1847, about 300,000 destitute Irish people were living in Liverpool. Some crowded into rooming houses, where, if they had any money at all, they often became victims of con men who took their coins in exchange for empty promises to help book them a spot on a ship. Others lived in unsanitary conditions on the streets. Disease spread quickly and killed many of the emigrants before they were able to leave England.

The English residents of Liverpool were appalled by this onslaught of the Irish poor. One editorial in the *Liverpool Mail* took Irish landlords to task for not providing for their impoverished tenants: "Instead of having the pride or the honesty to maintain their own poor, as the poorest parish in England does, they export them in ship-loads to prey upon the humanity of this country. This conduct is not only indecent, it is criminal and ought to be punished." The author, however, reserved plenty of contempt for the Irish emigrants themselves. His suggested remedy to the problem was to "[g]ive these beggars . . . a loaf of bread and send them home."[1]

ACROSS THE ATLANTIC

Some Irish emigrants decided to stay in England. Most of them headed inland and settled in industrial areas such as Birmingham and Manchester. A small group of about 14,000 headed to Australia, including 4,000 teenage girls who had been orphaned and left to the care of workhouses. Originally a prison colony, Australia welcomed the Irish girls because women were scarce there.

The most popular destinations, however, were Canada and the United States. Most emigrants wanted to go to the United States, but in 1847 about 45 percent of them went to Canada—

then still part of the British Empire—because the fare was substantially cheaper. But no matter where they were headed, the voyage across the Atlantic Ocean that year was difficult, if not deadly.

THE COFFIN SHIPS

In the spring of 1847, Stephen De Vere, an Irish member of Parliament, became alarmed by the horrific stories about the ships that were carrying desperate Irish emigrants to North America. To find out if the stories were true, he booked passage on a ship bound for Canada. His chilling eyewitness account of his journey, an excerpt of which appears below, helped convince the British Parliament to adopt stricter regulation of living conditions aboard these emigrant ships.

Before the Emigrant has been a week at sea he is an altered man. How can it be otherwise? Hundreds of poor people, men, women, and children; of all years from the drivelling idiot of 90 to the babe just born; huddled together without light, without air; wallowing in filth and breathing a fetid atmosphere; sick in body; dispirited in heart;—the fevered Patients lying between the Sound, in sleeping places so narrow as almost to deny them the power of indulging by a change of position the natural restlessness of the disease; by their agonized ravings disturbing those around, & predisposing them through the Effects of the imagination, to imbibe the contagion; living without food or medicine except as Administered by the hand of Casual charity; dying without the voice of Spiritual Consolation; and buried in the deep—without the rites of the Church. The food is generally ill selected and seldom in consequence of the insufficiency and bad construction of the cooking places. The supply of water

The trip took about a month. Passengers were packed into overcrowded and unsanitary cargo ships, many of which were in disrepair. The food that passengers were given to eat was sometimes rotten. Often they received little water, and what they did

hardly enough for cooking and drinking does not allow Washing. In many Ships the filthy beds teeming with all abominations are never required to be brought to Deck and aired;—the narrow space between the Sleeping berths & the piles of Boxes is never washed or scraped; but breathes up a damp and fetid stench, until the day before arrival at Quarantine when all hands are required to "Scrub Up", and put on a fair face for the Doctor and Government Inspector. . . . The meat was of the worst quality. The supply of Water shipped on board was abundant; but the quantity served out to the Passengers was so scanty that they were frequently obligated to throw overboard their Salt Provisions and Rices (a most important Article of their Food) because they had not water enough both for the necessary Cooking, and the satisfying of their raging thirst afterwards. . . .

Disease and Death among the Emigrants,—nay the propagation of Infection throughout Canada are not the worst consequences of this atrocious System of neglect, and ill usage. A result far worse is to be found in the utter demoralization of the Passengers both Male and Female, by the filth, debasement, and disease of two or three months so passed. The Emigrant enfeebled in body and degraded in mind even though he should have the physical power had not the , has not the to exert himself.—He has lost his self respect, his elasticity of Spirit.*

* "Right of Passage." Moving Here, Staying Here: The Canadian Immigrant Experience, Library and Archives Canada. http://www.collectionscanada.gc.ca/immigrants/021017-2113.03-e.html.

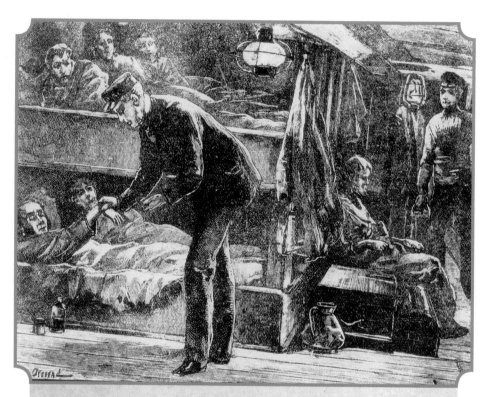

This 1846 illustration depicts Irish immigrants aboard a ship bound for the United States at the time of the Irish famine. Many immigrants risked their lives on overcrowded and unsanitary ships to make the journey.

get was frequently so polluted it was nearly undrinkable. These appalling conditions helped spread typhus and other diseases. So many people died on board that the vessels became known as "coffin ships." One expert, scholar Kerby Miller, estimates that, in 1847 alone, the death rate among Irish immigrants to the United States was 9 percent. The rate was even higher among those who went to Canada. Perhaps as many as 30 percent were victims of the coffin ships bound for that country.

TRAGEDY AT GROSSE ISLE

The appalling death rate for Canada was partly due to its quarantine policy. Immigrants had to enter Canada through two quarantine stations, one at Partridge Island for the province of New Brunswick and one at Grosse Isle for the province of Quebec. The stations were supposed to provide medical care for any sick passengers in order to keep them from spreading disease to the Canadian population.

At Grosse Isle, the facilities were tragically inadequate to deal with the flood of Irish immigrants, who began arriving en masse in May 1847. The hospitals on the island could accommodate just 2,000 patients—a mere fraction of the ailing passengers suffering from typhus, dysentery, and other ailments. By the end of the month, some 40 ships were clogging up the St. Lawrence River, as the Grosse Isle staff struggled to deal with the sick. Some of the ships were trapped in the river for days or even weeks. Healthy patients aboard started contracting disease, as they exhausted whatever supplies of food and water they had left. The legacy of the disaster at Grosse Isle is a mass grave stretching over six acres where more than 5,400 Irish immigrants were buried.

Such mass death forced the Canadian government to give up its efforts to quarantine sick immigrants. As feared, they set off a string of epidemics in cities such as Montreal, Quebec, and St. John's. One of the victims was John E. Mills, the mayor of Montreal. Before his death, he signed a petition, drafted by city leaders, to Queen Victoria. It called for the British government to put an end to Irish immigration to Canada. Revealing the same prejudices against the Irish that were prevalent in England, it called the Irish immigrants "paupers unused to labour, mendicants with large families, averse from every industrious pursuit, whole cargoes of human beings in a state of destitution and in every stage of disease."[2]

VIEWS OF EMIGRATION

Many Irish immigrants to the United States encountered similar hostility. Those who survived the trip were usually weak and malnourished. While still recovering from the famine years and their brutal ocean voyage, they were plunged into a new and unfamiliar world. Mostly illiterate and unskilled, the Irish struggled to fit into American society, which looked down on these ragged newcomers. Anti-Irish sentiment was exacerbated by Protestant Americans' uneasiness with Catholicism, the religion of most of the Irish immigrants. Hatred of the Irish and of Catholics became so widespread as to help the formation of a new political movement, known as the Know-Nothing Party, which was active in the 1840s and 1850s.

In Ireland, initially, most people viewed the mass emigration positively. They believed it offered emigrants a fresh chance in life, while at the same time reducing the number of people in Ireland struggling to get by with limited food sources. Priests encouraged people to emigrate, and the press praised landlords who financed their tenants' relocation abroad.

In late 1847, however, public opinion started to change. Irish journalists, politicians, and clergymen began to speak against emigration. Increasingly, they came to see it as a grand plot to steal Ireland from the Irish by depopulating the country. Those behind the plot were said to be the British government and the elite. Early on, the Irish had viewed the famine as a natural disaster, but as the crisis wore on and the government failed repeatedly to dip into its sizable coffers enough to end Irish suffering, many Irish began to wonder which was their greatest enemy: the blight or the English.

Eviction

In the summer of 1847, Charles Trevelyan reexamined the British government's relief policies in Ireland. Although the soup kitchens were a qualified success, he did not want to extend the food program past the September end date mandated by law. Like many officials, Trevelyan strongly believed that the soup kitchens were doing more harm than good because they eliminated the incentive for the Irish poor to work.

One element of the policy, however, had pleased him: its cost. The soup kitchens had been far less expensive than the relief works program they had replaced. In crafting a new relief policy, Trevelyan hoped to bring down the cost to the British taxpayer even more. His solution was to create a relief system in Ireland that would be entirely paid for by the Irish themselves.

The idea had the strong support of much of the English public. At first, English people had been extremely sympathetic to the plight of their Irish countrymen, but as the crisis continued, they experienced what is now often called "famine fatigue." Often in cases of famine, people in a position to help the victims become exhausted by pleas for aid. Worn down by terrible stories of suffering, they begin tuning out news of the disaster and sometimes even turn on the victims themselves, whom they blame for their inability to solve their own problems.

Many middle- and upper-class English people already held deep prejudices against the Irish, which helped them turn a blind eye to their plight. Most who harbored such biases were convinced that the Irish were a poor, backward people who did not really deserve sympathy or help. They told themselves that providing aid to Ireland was pointless because the problem with the Irish was far worse than a temporary famine. This line of thinking inspired a journalist for the *Times* of London to condemn Ireland as a "nation of beggars" and to conclude, "We have to change the very nature of a people born and bred, from time immemorial, in inveterate indolence, improvidence, disorder, and consequent destititution."[1] By seeing the famine as just a symptom of a much larger problem, they could congratulate themselves for any charity they gave to the Irish, even though it was clear that they were not giving enough to stave off mass death. This mind-set was highlighted in an article in the *Illustrated London News* published in November 1848:

> If the splendour of our benevolence has not kept pace with the hideousness of her [Ireland's] misery, it has not been from any want of inclination on the part of the living race of Englishmen, but from the sheer impossibility of remedying in one year the accumulated evils of ages, and of elevating the character of a people too poor and sorrow-stricken to attempt to elevate themselves.[2]

The English public reserved its most intense scorn for Irish landlords, who became a popular scapegoat for anyone with pangs of guilt for not doing enough for the starving Irish. Even though Ireland was part of their country, many English taxpayers claimed that famine relief was not their responsibility. Instead, they said, it was the obligation of the landlords to help their poor tenants. They also blamed the landlords for the recent onslaught of destitute and diseased Irish into Liverpool and other English cities. Rather than taking care of their own poor, the English claimed, the Irish landlords were sending them to English cities, where they would become the burden of the English people.

MAKING THE IRISH PAY

Such sentiments helped gain support for Trevelyan's new famine relief policy, which Parliament passed into law in June 1847. The Poor Law Extension Act set in motion the relief policies that the British government adhered to for the remainder of the famine. Provisions in the act planted the cost of relief completely on the shoulders of the Irish, and particularly on landlords. The British press described the law as an act of justice on behalf of the Irish poor. Now, newspapers explained, the landlords would be forced to do their Christian duty to the less fortunate. This high-minded justification ignored that the English had plenty to gain through the law: They no longer had to finance aid to a group of countrymen they did not particularly like.

Not surprisingly, the new law outraged the Irish landlords, who thought it was unfair that they should be expected to deal with such an enormous crisis without the help of the British Treasury. From a more practical standpoint, they claimed that it was impossible for them to do so. They, too, had been impoverished by the famine, because in many cases their tenants were completely without means to pay their rents. William Gregory, an Irish member of Parliament from Dublin, denounced the plan, insisting it was unrealistic given the scope of the crisis: "[T]he whole rental of Ireland would not suffice for the relief which must be required under this bill."[3]

But the press had no sympathy for the landlords. As the *Illustrated London News* jeered, "one would think they were the class to be pitied, not the famine-stricken peasantry."[4] The claim of some landlords that the high taxes would bankrupt them only made the law more appealing to many English people. Seeing the Irish landlords as lazy and immoral, they would be happy to see their Irish estates sold and placed into the hands of more deserving caretakers.

OUTDOOR RELIEF

According to the amended Poor Law, the money collected from Irish landlords would be used to pay for what was known as "outdoor relief." With the soup kitchens closing and the workhouses overflowing, the government developed a third program for helping people defined as the powerless poor. This class included the sick, old people, orphans, and widows with at least two legitimate children. They would be given food and allowed to live in their own homes.

The able-bodied could get relief only by seeking admittance to a workhouse. But if the local workhouse was full or experiencing an epidemic, they could receive outdoor relief as well. The able-bodied, however, would have to prove they were destitute by engaging in pointless hard labor, such as breaking stones with a hammer for hours at a time. The logic was that only the truly needy would submit themselves to this back-breaking humiliation instead of working a wage-paying job.

Providing outdoor relief was less expensive than expanding the workhouse system. Nevertheless, to keep costs down, officials did everything they could to discourage people from seeking relief. For instance, they restricted the number of stations where people could receive outdoor relief. The poor had to walk many miles, often in the rain and cold, to prove they were deserving of their meager rations. Officials also resisted distributing uncooked food or providing the poor with weekly, rather than daily, rations. Both measures were intended to make the outdoor relief system more efficient, but some officials feared they would encourage more people to seek relief.

THE GREGORY CLAUSE

The latest Poor Law contained another measure to help keep people off the relief roles. This was the quarter-acre clause, also known as the Gregory clause, after William Gregory, the Parliament member who pushed for it. It established that anyone who held more than a quarter of an acre of land was ineligible for the workhouse or for outdoor relief. Not only did it discourage the poor from seeking relief, it also helped landlords get rid of small landholders on their estates who likely no longer could afford to pay their rent. Only by forfeiting their land could these small holders receive the food they so desperately needed.

Sometimes, when tenants surrendered their holdings, landlords allowed them to dismantle their cabins and take the building materials with them. Wherever they ended up, they at least had a chance of avoiding homelessness. But few landlords were so generous. More often, if a tenant abandoned his land for the workhouse, the landlord immediately stripped off the cabin's roof. If the tenant returned, he found his old home uninhabitable.

Even with starvation looming, however, some proud landholders refused to give up their plots. For instance, a report to the poor-law commissioners recounted the story of Michael Bradley, who would not surrender his land in exchange for relief. He left his house, intending to travel to a nearby town to beg, but instead keeled over dead by the side of the road. The report noted that "such cases are . . . to be found in almost every district."[5]

FORCING PEOPLE FROM THEIR LAND

After the amendment of the Poor Act raised their taxes, landlords were desperate to remove from their lands any tenants not paying rent. In addition, they wanted to get rid of the poorest tenants, because the law required the landlord to pay their property taxes. Even if these tenants managed to pay their rent, the taxes were so high that the landlords lost money in the deal.

In the past, during lean years, if tenants fell behind in rent, the landlord often reduced their rent or allowed them to pay it at a later date. Although legally they could evict these tenants, landlords generally thought of eviction as an unwise business choice. It required too much effort and reaped too little reward. But now landlords saw eviction as an efficient way to rid themselves of nonpaying tenants who increased their tax burden. Even if tenants were up to date in their rent, landlords could refuse to extend their leases, placing the tenants in danger of eviction if they did not voluntarily leave their land holdings.

These evictions were completely legal. Moreover, the government implicitly supported the landlords' actions. Many officials hoped mass evictions would forever alter the system of land holding in Ireland. Why did they want this? In England, farms were generally larger and more productive than in Ireland. In fact, the "chock-a-block" system of subdividing Irish land into smaller and smaller units meant that English land produced twice as much in agriculture products than Irish land of the same acreage. Through the eviction of small landholders, both Irish landlords and British officials hoped that their land could be consolidated and sold to wealthy farmers who might make better use of it and could likely pay landlords higher rents. The rate of eviction began to explode in late 1847, and it remained high for many years.

Some indebted landlords turned to eviction only as a last resort. While a few offered their tenants small cash payments before they left their homes, many more treated their tenants brutally. This was especially true of absentee landlords, who neither knew their tenants nor had any interest in witnessing sobering scenes of starving families being ripped from the only homes they had ever known. With the support of some sheriffs, many landlords hired gangs to destroy their tenants' cabins to force them off the land and make sure they did not come back.

In this period illustration, members of an Irish peasant family unable to pay rent because of failure of the potato crop have been evicted from their home. Irish landlords were often merciless to their tenants during the famine.

Fearing violent retribution from their now-homeless tenants, landlords often arranged for a group of soldiers or policemen to oversee the process.

COPING WITH EVICTION

Once evicted, some tenants went to the workhouse or sought outdoor relief. Others were forced to beg or steal enough food to survive. The luckiest moved in with family and friends. Most, however, were forced to live in whatever makeshift shelter they could find. Exposed to the elements, many of the

THE MURDER OF MAJOR DENIS MAHON

The murder of Major Denis Mahon became an important news event during the famine years, one that illustrated to both the English and the Irish the simmering tensions between them.

Mahon was a former British army officer who went to County Roscommon in Ireland in 1835, having inherited a large estate near Strokestown. When the famine struck, Mahon became a member of the local relief committee. He often criticized Father Michael McDermott for his management of the area's soup kitchen.

To avoid having to pay taxes to fund the relief efforts, Mahon decided to pay for the emigration of his many tenants. In the summer of 1847, he hired a corrupt shipping agent to oversee the journey of 1,000 emigrants from his estate to Quebec, Canada, then the cheapest destination. For the emigrants, the trip was a disaster. About one-third of them died either on ship or soon after reaching Canada. But even this did not deter Mahon, who continued to push the rest of his tenants to leave Ireland.

On November 2, 1847, Mahon was returning home in his carriage after attending a meeting of the relief committee. A shot rang out, and Mahon fell dead. Within hours, his tenants were burning bonfires to celebrate his murder.

homeless fell victim to starvation and disease. One official described their suffering:

> [The evicted] betake themselves to the ditches or the shelter of some bank, and there exist like animals till starvation or the inclemency of the weather drives them to the workhouse.

The assassination made headlines in England and Ireland. Two men were subsequently arrested, tried, and executed for the crime. Newspapers and later accounts suggested various motives, but clearly Mahon's emigration schemes had made him an unpopular figure in Strokestown.

The Mahon case also highlighted a growing battle between the British government and the Irish clergy over the issues of emigration and eviction. In a public letter to Archbishop John MacHale, the Earl of Shrewsbury accused Father McDermott of inciting the violence. He claimed McDermott had spoken out against Mahon in a sermon the Sunday before the killing. McDermott subsequently proved he had not called for Mahon's death. MacHale wrote his own public letter in response to the accusation, in which he defended the role of priests in helping famine victims while lambasting English politicians for their seeming indifference to Irish suffering. Dripping with sarcasm, MacHale addressed the idea that the Irish were insufficiently grateful for the actions of the English government: "How ungrateful of the Catholics of Ireland not to pour forth canticles of gratitude to the [government] ministers, who promised that none of them should perish and then suffered [allowed] a million to starve."*

* James S. Donnelly, *The Great Irish Potato Famine*. Stroud, Gloucestershire: Sutton, 2001, p. 143.

Lord John Russell served as prime minister of Great Britain during the bulk of the Irish famine and presided over his government's ineffectual response to the humanitarian crisis. Many historians today regard him as one of the villains of the crisis.

There were three cartloads of these creatures, who could not walk, brought for admission yesterday, some in fever, some suffering from dysentery, and all from want of food.[6]

The rate of eviction was not uniform throughout Ireland. Generally, the poorer the region, the more often evictions occurred. The south and west had the most people dependent on the workhouse and outdoor relief. As a result, the taxes on landlords there were extraordinarily high, which in turn encouraged them to evict remaining tenants to lessen their financial hardships. County Clare was notorious for its high rate of evictions. Between 1849 and 1854, one of every 10 residents lost their land and homes. During this same period, some 49,000 families throughout Ireland endured the horrors of eviction.

On large estates, dozens of households were often evicted at the same time. Entire villages simply disappeared from the map. As activist John Mitchel later explained, "Whole neighbourhoods were often thrown out upon the highways in winter, and the homeless creatures lived for a while upon the charity of neighbours; but this was dangerous, for the neighbours were often themselves ejected for harbouring them."[7]

FIGHTING BACK

Weakened by famine, most evictees offered no resistance when they were driven out of their homes. But a small minority did commit acts of violence to protest the evictions. After seven landlords were shot in late 1847, a wave of panic spread among Irish landowners. Following an aggressive lobbying campaign, Parliament passed the Crime and Outrage Act in December 1847, which increased the number of government soldiers in Ireland and added regulations pertaining to who could legally carry firearms.

Prime Minister John Russell, however, was far from sympathetic to the landlords' plight. He said the shootings should not have been a surprise after landlords had "turn[ed] out fifty persons at once and burn[ed] their houses over their heads, giving them no provision for the future."[8] Russell urged lawmakers to outlaw the evictions.

A law regarding evictions did pass Parliament, but members of the House of Lords, many of whom were landlords themselves, watered down its toughest provisions. The legislation made it slightly more expensive for a landlord to evict his tenants. Landlords also could be charged with a misdemeanor if they tore down a tenant's house, but only if the tenants were inside at the time. Evictions had to take place during daylight, and none were permitted on Good Friday or Christmas. Such provisions, scant as they were, provided little comfort to starving family members forced to watch as a gang hired by their landlord, acting fully with his legal rights, tore down their house on December 26.

The Later Years

D uring the famine years, the news from Ireland was almost unrelentingly grim. One of the few bright moments came in the fall of 1847. After two years of potato harvests plagued with the blight, the potato crop—due to a warm, dry growing season—was finally disease-free.

Declaring the crisis at an end, Trevelyan confidently went ahead with his plan to dismantle the soup kitchens. Unfortunately for the starving Irish, the harvest proved extremely disappointing even without the blight. Only a small amount of acreage had been planted—just about 11 percent of what had been planted in 1845—so the healthy crop did little to end the famine. There were many reasons for such a small crop, including the fact that many farmers had to neglect their fields because their laborers were working at relief jobs. But the most significant factor for the small harvest was a lack of seed potatoes, which the government had made no effort to supply. Even when seed potatoes were planted, the starving often dug them up and ate them in their desperation to stay alive.

Still, the blight-free harvest was a cause for optimism. It inspired farmers to plant as much land as they could the next year. But all hope for the famine's end vanished when once again the blight returned. The anemic harvest of 1848 was only half of the previous year's crop. Adding to Ireland's miseries, the grain harvest was also exceptionally low.

THE YOUNG IRELANDERS

The summer of 1848 saw a series of rebellions throughout Europe. These revolts inspired a group of Irish activists called the Young Irelanders. Before the famine, they had fought to repeal the Act of Union, which had placed Ireland under the control of the British Parliament. They wanted Ireland to become an independent nation, with its own lawmaking body.

When the famine hit, the Young Irelanders saw support for their cause dwindle. People who now worried about where their next meal was coming from had little interest in the group's revolutionary rhetoric. The British government, however, was concerned that the suffering of the Irish might inspire a political revolt. Hoping to discourage any resurgence of interest in the Young Irelanders, it arrested and tried three of its leaders—William Smith O'Brien, Thomas Francis Meagher, and John Mitchel—for treason in May 1848. Hung juries released O'Brien and Meagher, while Mitchel, in a corrupt trial, was found guilty and sent to a penal colony in Australia.

Rather than discouraging the core members of the Young Irelanders, the trials invigorated them. They believed that finally the time was right to battle the powers of the British government. If they began a revolution, they reasoned, the miserable Irish would surely be inspired to join them.

Without much of a plan, the rebels made their move on July 30, 1848. Led by Smith O'Brien, about 40 of them, joined by

100 peasants armed with stones, confronted a group of police in the town of Ballingarry in County Tipperary. The revolt fell apart almost as soon as it began. The police killed several of the rebels before a contingent of troops arrived and put down the rebellion completely. O'Brien managed to escape. He later wrote angrily about the Irish poor's unwillingness to join his cause: "[T]he people preferred to die of starvation at home, or to flee as voluntary exiles to other lands, rather than to fight for their lives and liberties."[1]

The English newspapers poked fun of the Young Irelanders' failed revolt. The *Times* of London, for instance, mocked it as the "cabbage-garden revolution"[2] because much of the fighting took place in the garden of an old widow. However brief, the Battle of Ballingarry did have several important effects. In the short run, it discouraged political unrest among the Irish. As former prime minister Robert Peel wrote, "Smith O'Brien has rendered more service [to the English government] than I thought he was capable of rendering by making rebellion ridiculous."[3]

CHARITY DRIES UP

For much of the English public, the failed revolt also seemed to prove their worse prejudices about the Irish. Now they felt fully justified in characterizing the Irish as not only lazy and backward, but also as hideously ungrateful. Ever eager to see themselves as generous in their aid to Ireland during the famine, many English people decided that they had done too much to help the hopelessly immoral Irish. Prime Minister John Russell summed up these sentiments: "We have subscribed, worked, visited, clothed, for the Irish, millions of money, years of debate, etc., etc., etc. The only return is rebellion and calumny. Let us not grant, lend, clothe, etc., any more, and see what that will do . . . British people think this."[4]

In the wake of the Battle of Ballingarry, public and private charity toward the Irish began to dry up. The government was

(continues on page 94)

JOHN MITCHEL

Irish journalist and activist John Mitchel famously wrote, "The Almighty, indeed, sent the potato blight, but the English created the famine."* His writings helped promote the idea that British policy during the famine was designed to exterminate the Irish poor.

The son of a Presbyterian minister, Mitchel was born in County Londonderry on November 3, 1815. He probably attended Trinity College and briefly practiced law. In 1843, he became involved in the nationalist movement, which sought Ireland's independence from the British government. Two years later, Mitchel began writing for the *Nation*, a nationalist newspaper. In February 1848, he left the *Nation* to establish his own paper, the *United Irishman*, in which he called on the Irish to win their freedom through armed revolution. A month later, Mitchel was arrested and charged with treason. In a rigged trial, he was convicted and sentenced to 14 years in a prison colony in Australia.

In 1853, Mitchel escaped and made his way to the United States. He settled in New York, where his writings were already popular in the Irish-American community. There he established the *Citizen*. His newspaper frequently courted controversy, most notably when, while feuding with prominent abolitionists, he came out in favor of slavery in the American South. Enchanted with southern life, Mitchel moved to Tennessee. During the U.S. Civil War (1861-1865), he strongly supported the Confederacy. Because of his pro-South writings, Mitchel was briefly imprisoned after the Confederacy lost the war.

During the 1850s and 1860s, Mitchel also wrote several books about Ireland's relations with Britain. They included

John Mitchel was an ardent Irish patriot, activist, solicitor, and political journalist, who laid the blame of the potato famine directly at the feet of the British government. He was a key member of the revolutionary groups Young Ireland and the Irish Confederation.

Jail Journal (1854), *The Last Conquest of Ireland (Perhaps)* (1858), *An Apology for the British Government in Ireland* (1860), and *History of Ireland* (1868). Especially in *The Last Conquest*, Mitchel vilified the British government for its inaction during the Great Irish Famine. Passionate and bitter, the book made the case that British elites engineered the mass death of the Irish in order to take control of Irish land.

Mitchel returned to Ireland in 1875. He successfully ran for Parliament, but the government voided the election on the grounds that Mitchel was a convicted felon. The voters elected Mitchel a second time, but before the matter was resolved, Mitchel died on March 20, 1875.

---

* John Mitchel, *The Last Conquest of Ireland (Perhaps)*. Glasgow: R. & T. Washbourne, 1858, p. 219.

(continued from page 91)
happy to have an excuse to ignore the continuing suffering in Ireland. Likewise, the English public, suffering from an economic downturn, were pleased to have a reason not to feel guilty about not contributing toward Irish relief. Even the Quakers began to waver in their commitment to help the starving. Their officials were exhausted, both emotionally and financially, by the seemingly never-ending Irish crisis.

Some other religious groups stepped in to offer the aid the Quakers were no longer able to provide. Among them was a group of Anglicans who operated a mission on Achill Island in County Mayo. Led by the clergyman Edward Nangle, they provided soup to hundreds of poor Irish, but only after they abandoned Catholicism and converted to Anglicanism. Although these conversions were rarely sincere, Nangle saw them as proof that God had caused the famine to destroy Catholicism. Forcing religion conversions in exchange for food became known as "Souperism." While there were in fact relatively few incidences of Souperism, in Ireland they became an important part of the popular folklore that grew out of the famine.

THE SCOURGE OF CHOLERA

Just as charity for the Irish was growing scarcer, they were hit by another heavy blow. In December 1848, an epidemic of Asiatic cholera broke out in a Belfast workhouse. Within a month, the disease had spread throughout Ireland. Cholera terrified the population with its ability to kill its victims swiftly. After contracting the disease, people could die in a matter of days. In some cases, victims lived with cholera no more than a few hours. The epidemic did not end until the summer of 1850, by which time it had killed at least 36,000 Irish.

Cholera helped make 1849 the worst year of the famine. In the south and west, the poor-law unions, which administered the government's relief, could no longer raise enough funds to help the starving and ill. Yet the government still refused to provide Ireland with additional aid, instead insisting that all relief be financed through taxes on Irish landholders. Edward Twisleton, a member of the Poor Law Commission, was so disgusted by the government's unwillingness to address the growing crisis that he resigned his post. As his resignation explained, "the destitution here [in Ireland] is so horrible, and the indifference of the House of Commons to it so manifest, that he is an unfit agent of a policy that must be one of extermination."[5]

Charles Trevelyan did, however, deal with the bankruptcy of the poor-law unions in the most overburdened areas. In the past, each union was supposed to be financed through local taxes. Trevelyan proposed to change this through his "rate-in-aid" plan. It called for tax income to be evenly distributed throughout Ireland, with the wealthier areas subsidizing the poorer ones. The plan ensured that even the few relatively prosperous areas of Ireland—the provinces of Leinster and Ulster—would be economically devastated by the continuing famine.

THE ENCUMBERED ESTATES ACT

In July 1849, the British government made another controversial decision. By passing the Encumbered Estates Act, Parliament made it easier to force Irish landlords to sell their lands to pay off their debts. The law was designed to bankrupt the hated Irish landlords and place their estates in the hands of new landowners, who in the eyes of the government would manage the properties in a more responsible manner.

The act all at once placed large areas of Irish land on the market. As a result, the price of land plummeted. Even Irish landlords who did not have large debts suddenly faced bankruptcy, because their land lost much of its value virtually overnight. Land speculators rushed in to snap up bargains that they could later resell for huge profits. For instance, Vincent Scully, an Irish member of Parliament, bought the Castle Hyde estate in County Cork for £14,425 in 1851. Just nine years later, he sold it for £45,000. The English elite hoped that once the old Irish landlords were cleared out, they would be replaced with English and Scottish landlords. The *Times* of London predicted, "In a few years more, a Celtic Irishman will be as rare in Connemara [in County Galway] as is the Red Indian on the shores of Manhattan."[6] In the end, however, wealthy Irishmen purchased most of the available land. Between October 1849 and August 1857, only about 14 percent of Irish land was bought by non-Irish.

Another effect of the Encumbered Estates Act was a spike in evictions. The new owners who took over Irish estates did not feel any more obligation toward their poor tenants than most of the old ones had. In fact, the new landlords usually just wanted to clear out the tenants as quickly as possible. Much of Ireland was ideal for raising livestock. Rather than farm their estates, these landlords wanted to convert their land to pastures where animals could graze.

A VISIT FROM VICTORIA

Just a month after the Encumbered Estates Act was passed, Victoria, the queen of the United Kingdom of Britain and Ireland, arrived in Ireland. The visit was meant to reassure the Irish people that the British government and people had not forgotten them. Despite the anti-English sentiments then widespread in Ireland, many Irish still felt a fondness for the queen. Wherever she went, crowds gathered just to catch a glimpse of her.

During the visit, Queen Victoria tried to assure the Irish that she felt sorrow over their troubles and wished for their well-being. In one speech she said, "I have felt deeply for their sufferings, and it will be a source of heartfelt satisfaction to me if I am permitted to witness the future and lasting prosperity of this portion of the United Kingdom."[7] But whatever thought Queen Victoria had given to the Irish and their suffering, seeing them line the streets to greet her still gave her shock. In a

"DOTH NOT A MEETING LIKE THIS MAKE AMENDS?"
H—R M—J—Y THE Q—N. "MY DEAR IRELAND, HOW MUCH BETTER YOU LOOK SINCE MY LAST VISIT. I AM SO GLAD!"

In August 1861, Queen Victoria, together with other members of the royal family, landed at Kingstown in Ireland for their third visit of her reign. This was the first time the British monarch had come to Ireland since the famine.

letter to her uncle, the queen wrote, "You see more ragged and wretched people here than I ever saw anywhere else."[8]

Hoping to make sure that the queen understood their plight as well as she said she did, evictees from the town of Kilrush sent Victoria a speech during the royal visit. Just as Skibbereen had become a symbol of the horrors of the famine early on, Kilrush was an emblem of the miseries attended by eviction. Between 1847 and 1850, an astounding 17 percent of Kilrush's residents had been thrown out of their homes.

In the address, the evictees took the British government to task not only for its failure to help the Irish, but also for making their plight worse through supporting the evictions:

> Madam, in no other region of the habitable globe would it be permitted to two or three satraps [government officials], however specious of the pretences of law or custom which they might allege, to unroof and demolish at their pleasure the homes of fifteen thousand human beings, and to turn out that multitude, in itself a nation, to die by the slow wasting of famine and disease.[9]

The Kilrush evictees also reminded the queen that what had happened in Ireland would not soon be forgotten, but would live on in memory as one of her legacies. "[T]hy royal name," they wrote, "must be connected in future history with the astounding record of the extermination of our unhappy race."[10]

Legacy of the Great Irish Famine

Historians dispute the precise year that marked the end of the Great Irish Famine. Some cite it as 1850; others, 1852. Whatever the exact end date, it was clear that the worst was over by the early 1850s. The blight still damaged the annual potato crop from time to time, but never with the ferocity that it had during the years of the famine. Its effect on Irish agriculture was further diminished in the 1880s, when farmers discovered that spraying a solution of copper sulphate on their potato stalks could kill the blight and save their crops.

But while the famine came to an end, its legacy lived on. The event had been such a catastrophe for the Irish that it left all of Ireland profoundly changed. Indeed, scholars still often divide Irish history into the pre-famine years and the post-famine years.

A POPULATION DECLINE

One of the most important changes brought on by the famine was a dramatic drop in the Irish population. The Irish census of 1841 placed Ireland's population at about 8.2 million. The population was rising in the early 1840s, so when the blight first began to take its toll, the number of people in Ireland was probably closer to 8.5 million. When the next census was taken in 1851, it revealed that the population had dropped to 6.6 million. Some of the decrease was probably due to a low birth rate. A people weak and malnourished do not have as many children as they would have otherwise. But most of the drop is attributed to two other factors—death and emigration.

Because of the chaos of the famine years, there are no definitive records about how many people died and their cause of death. Although estimates by modern historians vary, probably at least one million people perished during the famine. While some died of starvation, the majority probably fell victim to epidemic disease. These deaths were not distributed evenly throughout Ireland. Poorer regions in the south and west were hit much harder than other areas. The provinces with the highest death rates were Connacht and Munster, where about one in every four people died. Death was also more prevalent among certain segments of the population. The very old and the very young were the most vulnerable. These groups accounted for three-fifths of all deaths. Poverty also increased a person's chance of dying, but the middle class and even the wealthy were often not saved from death from disease.

At least another million Irish left Ireland during the famine. After surviving a perilous journey, they built new lives in England, Australia, Canada, and the United States. In most cases, these emigrants never again saw their native homeland.

LAND REFORMS

The natural outgrowth of the massive and sudden population drop in Ireland was a change in its system of land ownership.

Before the famine, landlords and their agents divided estates into small farms. Farmers further subdivided the land into tiny plots, each worked by a laborer and his family. The English elite had long bemoaned this convoluted system, which they claimed made it impossible to make the most of Ireland's best lands.

For them, the famine was seen as a blessing. In only a matter of years, the traditional method of landownership had been ripped apart. The old Irish landlords went bankrupt, agents were edged out of their roles as middlemen, small farmers with means abandoned their lands to emigrate, and poor tenants died or were evicted. Suddenly, the new landlords who bought up the bankrupt and depopulated estates allowed Irish land to be consolidated into larger, more economically productive farms and pastures. That their good fortune resulted from the misery and death of millions did not keep them from celebrating it. As a land agent and speculator named William Steuart Trench wrote, "Nothing but the successive failures of the potato . . . could have produced the emigration which will, I trust, give us room to become civilised."[1]

Irish agricultural workers who survived the famine were not so pleased with this turn of events. They often loathed the new landlords, who seemed to have benefited so greatly from the disaster. Throughout the late nineteenth and early twentieth centuries, tensions between laborers and landlords repeatedly erupted into violence. These protests encouraged the British government to enact a series of laws that essentially put an end to absentee landlords and allowed for some tenants to gain ownership of the lands they occupied.

Despite these reforms, many people in Ireland continued to live from hand to mouth. Letters from relatives who had emigrated earlier convinced many to look for new lives far from their homeland. Long after the famine, emigration continued to be an important part of Irish life. For the remainder of the nineteenth century, about half the people of each generation born in Ireland decided to emigrate. By 1910, more than 5 million Irish lived outside of Ireland.

MEMORIES OF THE FAMINE

Both in Ireland and in Irish immigrant communities abroad, memories about the famine lived on long after the damage done

THE FAMINE AND IRISH INDEPENDENCE

Before the Great Irish Famine, political activists in Ireland had pushed for the repeal of the Act of Union, which placed Ireland under the control of the British Parliament. During the famine years, interest in this nationalist movement waned as the Irish were too weak and traumatized to think about anything beyond their own survival. By the 1850s, however, as the famine ended, the cause of Irish independence reemerged. Inflamed by their anger over the British government's limited response to the famine, activists were more passionate than ever in their quest for freedom from British rule.

Following the failed uprising in 1848, members of the Young Irelanders, a nationalist group, evaded prosecution by escaping to the United States. There, one of them, John O'Mahony, founded the Fenian Brotherhood in 1848. Ten years later, nationalist James Stephens founded the Irish Republican Brotherhood (IRB). Sinn Féin, another important nationalist group, was established in Ireland in 1905.

The late nineteenth century also saw a movement to pressure the British government to grant Irish Home Rule; that is, the right for Ireland to rule itself through its own parliament. Central to this battle was Charles Stewart Parnell, who, as a member of the British Parliament in the late nineteenth century, led the Irish Parliamentary Party.

by the blight. People who had survived the famine told stories of what they had lived through to their children and grand-children, who then passed on these sad tales to later generations.

The party was instrumental in the passage of the Third Home Rule Act of 1914. It called for the establishment of a separate Irish government, but its creation was delayed with the outbreak of World War I (1914-1918).

Sinn Féin rebels seeking complete independence for Ireland revolted in 1916 during the Easter Rising. British soldiers crushed the rebellion, but their brutality only increased the support for the rebels' cause. Sinn Féin leaders won a majority of Ireland's parliamentary seats, and in 1919 they declared that the island of Ireland was now the independent Irish Republic. A two-year guerrilla war followed, which pitted the Irish Republican Army against British soldiers. The war ended with the signing of the Anglo-Irish Treaty. Through this agreement, the Irish Republic became the Irish Free State. The treaty also allowed six counties in the northern part of Ireland, which was home to many Protestants, to choose to leave the Catholic-dominated Irish Free State and remain part of Britain. This area is now known as Northern Ireland, which with England, Scotland, and Wales makes up the modern United Kingdom.

The Irish Free State was not fully independent. It was still part of the British Commonwealth. Amid years of political turmoil, however, the Irish continued to move toward greater freedom. In 1937, the country renamed itself Ireland and adopted a new constitution. Finally, in 1949, through the Republic of Ireland Act, the country severed its ties to the British monarch and became a democratic republic. The Republic of Ireland is today the home of approximately 4.6 million people.

One hundred years after the famine, the Irish Folklore Commission collected these oral histories. This collection of memories reveals many shared traumas from the time—from the terror of being evicted to the horror of not being able to bury loved ones properly to the gratitude of starving people upon receiving much needed aid from charitable groups.

Also well imprinted into the public memory of the famine was the failure of the British government to provide adequate help for the suffering Irish. For decades afterward, one specific complaint against the government became almost mythically important in the Irish psyche—that the government continued to allow the exportation of food grown in Ireland while the poor Irish were starving. Fifty years after the famine, Irish scholar Canon Peter O'Leary encapsulated the bitterness the Irish still felt over the issue of the exports in his memoirs:

> There was sent out from Ireland that year [1846] as much—no! twice as much—corn as would have nourished every person living in the country. The harbours of Ireland were full of ships and the ships full of Irish corn; they were leaving the harbours while the people were dying with the hunger throughout the land.[2]

Many modern scholars, however, note that even if the government had halted food exports, the famine would have still been devastating to Ireland. Some have also pointed out that, after 1846, the food imports into Ireland were substantially greater than the food exports shipped out of it.

The government's seeming indifference to Ireland's plight also gave rise to the notion that the British consciously used the crisis of the famine to destroy the Irish people—an idea popularized by Irish activist and journalist John Mitchel in his 1858 book, *The Last Conquest of Ireland (Perhaps)*. Mitchel claimed that the disaster was an artificial famine created by the government to exterminate the Irish in what would today be called genocide. He wrote, "Now, that million and a half of men, women, and children, were carefully, prudently, and peacefully slain by the English government. They died of hunger in the midst of abundance, which their own hands created."[3]

Mitchel was just one of many anti-English activists who used anger over the famine to promote the cause of Irish nationalism. Convinced like Mitchel that the famine was created by the government's actions, they often refused to call it a famine at all. They referred to it as the "great starvation" or the "great hunger."[4] By politicizing the famine as a symbol of the tyranny of British rule over Ireland, nationalists drew many more of the Irish to their cause.

THE FAMINE AS HISTORY

In the 1930s, some historians began to challenge the idea that British policy during the famine era amounted to an act of genocide against the Irish people. These scholars, most of whom studied history in England, were called revisionists because they were trying to revise the popular histories of the period. One of the most important revisionist texts was *The Great Famine: Studies in Irish History, 1845–52*, published in 1956. The book defended the actions of the British government, suggesting that its politicians and bureaucrats had done the best they could to deal with an incredibly difficult situation. As the preface explained, "In folklore and political writings the failure of the British government to act in a generous manner is quite understandably seen in a sinister light, but the private papers and the labours of genuinely good men tell an additional story. There was no conspiracy to destroy the Irish nation."[5]

In 1962, a popular historian named Cecil Woodham-Smith challenged the revisionist view. Her book *The Great Hunger: Ireland, 1845–1849* was a bestseller in both the United States and Europe. Although Woodham-Smith used much more measured language than John Mitchel, she too condemned the British government for doing far too little to help the Irish.

Many other historians have since taken up the anti-revisionist banner. For instance, A.J.P. Taylor, in an important article published in the journal *Irish Historical Studies*, placed much of the blame for Irish suffering at the feet of policy architects John Russell and Charles Trevelyan: "They were gripped by the most horrible, and perhaps the most universal, of human maladies: the belief that principles and doctrines are more important than lives. They imagined that rules, invented by economists, were as 'natural' as the potato blight."[6]

COMMEMORATING THE FAMINE

Both scholarly and popular interest in the Great Irish Famine exploded in the early 1990s, as its one hundred fiftieth anniversary approached. This newfound fascination in the event was a stark contrast to the hundredth anniversary in the 1940s, when few commemorations had been planned. At the time, the children of some famine victims were still alive, so the pain of the era was relatively fresh. Also, in at least some cases, relatives of those who survived might have been reluctant to confront the less-than-heroic measures—such as stealing or hoarding food—they took to save their lives. By the 1990s, however, enough time had passed that many people both in Ireland and in Irish communities abroad wanted to reassess Ireland's great national trauma.

To explore ways of properly commemorating the famine, the Irish government appointed a Famine Committee in 1994. In addition to funding new historical research, it organized the government's official commemorations, which culminated in the summer of 1997 with a music festival. Some criticized the festival for not showing the proper respect for the famine victims. Others objected to the government ending its anniversary observations in 1997, because it implied the famine ended in 1847, when in fact food shortages and related deaths continued for several more years.

At one of the 1997 commemorations, held in County Cork, Prime Minister Tony Blair issued the first formal apology by the British government for its actions during the Great Irish Famine. Irish actor Gabriel Byrne read the statement to a crowd of 15,000. "The famine was a defining event in the history of Ireland and Britain," Blair's statement read. "It has left deep scars. That one million people should have died in what was then part of the richest and most powerful nation in the world is something that still causes pain as we reflect on it today. Those who governed in London at the time failed their people."[7] Prime Minister John Bruton of Ireland praised Blair's apology: "While the statement confronts the past honestly, it does so in a way that heals for the future."[8]

MEMORIALS FOR THE VICTIMS

Several museums in Ireland operate as permanent memorials to the famine victims. The mansion at Strokestown, where landlord Denis Mahon was murdered during the famine, is now a museum and archive, which houses one of the largest collections about the era. In County Laois, the Donaghmore Famine Workhouse Museum allows visitors to experience how workhouse residents lived during and after the famine. In many Irish towns and cities, public sculptures also remind people of the most tragic event in Irish history. Perhaps the best known is erected at the Custom House Quays in Dublin. Created by artist Rowan Gillespie, the sculpture depicts several skeletal figures representing the many famine victims who emigrated from Dublin's port.

Outside of Ireland, famine memorials are found wherever Irish immigrants settled. In England, a plaque on the gates at Clarence Dock in Liverpool commemorates the more than one million Irish people who came to the city to board emigrant ships after the blight first struck. In Australia, a monument in the Hyde Parks Barracks in Sydney is dedicated to the Irish

Today, there are numerous memorials all around the world commemorating the victims of the Irish famine. One of the most moving can be found on the Custom House Quay in Dublin, where thousands of Irish boarded ships to leave their homeland for good during the famine years.

orphan girls who came there in the late 1840s. In Canada, Grosse Isle, where thousands of Irish immigrants perished in the summer of 1847, is a national historic site.

In the United States, memorials and sculptures have been erected in many areas that have large Irish-American populations, including Boston, Massachusetts; Chicago, Illinois; Fairfield, Connecticut; Portland, Oregon; Providence, Rhode Island; Rochester, New York; and Philadelphia, Pennsylvania. In New York City, the entry point for the majority of famine immigrants, the Irish Hunger Memorial was dedicated in 2002. Stretching over one-quarter acre (recalling the notorious quarter-acre clause of the 1847 poor-law amendment), the memorial features a landscape design that incorporates stones and plants from Ireland. Also on the site is an Irish cottage, imported from County Mayo.

REMEMBERING SKIBBEREEN

To acknowledge the importance of the Great Irish Famine, the Irish government declared that starting in 2009 one day a year would be set aside as a National Famine Memorial Day. Although commemorations would be held throughout Ireland, one location would be chosen each year to host a series of events to help the Irish remember and honor those lost to the famine. Choosing the first such location was hardly difficult. It made sense to all that the primary commemoration ceremonies should be held in Skibbereen—the little town that, for more than 150 years, has been synonymous with the worst horrors of the famine.

In mid-May 2009, thousands of visitors arrived in Skibbereen. They attended lectures on the latest scholarship on the famine as well as musical and theatrical events that explored the national trauma it had caused. Visitors took walking tours of the town to see sites described in journalistic accounts of Skibbereen in 1847, the year the extent of the scope of the disaster first became fully understood by the world outside. At the week's end, on May 17, the visitors and residents of Skibbereen joined with the rest of their nation to observe a minute of silence. As the seconds ticked away, all of Ireland contemplated the nation's great tragedy, alone and together reflecting on the horror unleashed when this natural disaster was met with considerable human indifference.

1801   The Act of Union creates the United Kingdom of Great Britain and Ireland.

1834   The Poor Law Amendment Act calls for the establishment of workhouses for the poor.

1845   September The first reports surface that the blight has contaminated Ireland's potato crop.

October Prime Minister Robert Peel establishes the Scientific Commission.

TIMELINE

1845
September The first reports surface that the blight has contaminated Ireland's potato crop.
November Prime Minister Robert Peel secretly purchases Indian corn from the United States to help feed the Irish poor.

1845 — 1846

1846
August The new British prime minister, John Russell, announces plans to halt food distribution in Ireland and replace it with a relief works program.
October Starving Irish in Dungarvan stage a riot to protest the exportation of food.

November Peel secretly purchases Indian corn from the United States to help feed the Irish poor; the Relief Commission meets for the first time.

1846   **March** Government-run food depots begin distributing Indian corn in Ireland.

August The new British prime minister, John Russell, announces plans to halt food distribution in Ireland and replace it with a relief works program.

October Starving Irish in Dungarvan stage a riot to protest the exportation of food.

1847
February The British Parliament passes a law calling for the creation of temporary soup kitchens throughout Ireland.
June The Poor Law Extension Act requires the Irish to pay for all famine relief.

1851

1847

2009

1848
December An epidemic of Asiatic cholera begins with an outbreak in a Belfast workhouse.

1850
The Great Irish Famine comes to an end.

2009
The first National Famine Memorial Day is observed in Skibbereen.

1847   **January** The British Association for the Relief of the Extreme Distress in Ireland and Scotland is established.

February The British Parliament passes a law calling for the creation of temporary soup kitchens throughout Ireland; James Mahony reports in the *Illustrated London News* about famine conditions in Skibbereen in County Cork.

April The Irish Fever Act establishes temporary fever hospitals to cope with disease epidemics; the British government sets up its model soup kitchen in Dublin.

May Dozens of ships of Irish emigrants overwhelm the quarantine station at Grosse Isle in Canada.

June The Poor Law Extension Act requires the Irish to pay for all famine relief, allows for the ill and indigent to receive food without living in a workhouse, and excludes land holders with more than one-quarter acre from receiving relief.

November Landlord Denis Mahon is murdered after forcing thousands of tenants to immigrate to Canada.

1848   **May** Three Young Irelander activists are arrested and charged with treason by the British government.

July Irish rebels stage an ill-fated attempt to revolt against British rule in the Battle of Ballingarry.

December An epidemic of Asiatic cholera begins with an outbreak in a Belfast workhouse.

1849   **July** The Encumbered Estates Act makes it easier to force bankrupt Irish landlords to sell their estates to pay their debts.

August Queen Victoria pays a royal visit to Ireland.

1850   The Great Irish Famine comes to an end.

1851   The Irish census claims that, in the past 10 years, the Irish population has dropped from 8.2 million to 6.6 million.

1921   The Anglo-Irish Treaty gives Ireland independenece in its home affairs, though the country remains loyal to the British crown.

1922   The Irish Free State is established as a dominion under British soverignty and remains so until 1937.

1945   The Irish Folklore Commission preserves recollections of the famine.

1949   The Republic of Ireland is established and the country withdraws from the British Commonwealth.

1997   The Irish government commemorates the one hundred fiftieth anniversary of the Great Irish Famine.

2009   The first National Famine Memorial Day is observed in Skibbereen.

NOTES

CHAPTER 1

1. James Mahony, "Sketches in the West of Ireland," *Illustrated London News*, February 13, 1847. http://adminstaff.vassar .edu/sttaylor/FAMINE/ILN/ West/West.html.
2. Ibid.
3. Ibid.
4. Ibid.
5 Ibid.
6. Ibid.
7. Ibid.
8. Ibid.
9. Ibid.
10. James Mahony, "Sketches in the West of Ireland," *Illustrated London News*, February 20, 1847. http://adminstaff.vassar .edu/sttaylor/FAMINE/ILN/ West/West2.html.
11. Ibid.
12. Ibid.
13. Ibid.
14. Ibid.
15. Ibid.
16. Ibid.
17. Ibid.

CHAPTER 2

1. Noel Kissane, *The Irish Famine: A Documentary History*. Dublin: National Library of Ireland, 1995, p. 3.

CHAPTER 3

1. Kissane, *The Irish Famine*, p. 21.
2. Ibid.

3. Ibid.
4. Ibid., p. 29.
5. James S. Donnelly, *The Great Irish Potato Famine*. Stroud, Gloucestershire: Sutton, 2001, p. 46.
6. Kissane, *The Irish Famine*, p. 37.
7. Ibid., p. 38.
8. Donnelly, *The Great Irish Potato Famine*, p. 51.
9. Kissane, *The Irish Famine*, p. 100.

CHAPTER 4

1. Kissane, *The Irish Famine*, p. 46.
2. Ibid.
3. Ibid., p. 125.
4. Ibid., p. 18.
5. Ibid., p. 48.
6. Donnelly, *The Great Irish Potato Famine*, p. 69.
7. Kissane, *The Irish Famine*, p. 55.
8. Ibid., p. 67.
9. Donnelly, *The Great Irish Potato Famine*, p. 78.
10. Kissane, *The Irish Famine*, p. 68.
11. Ibid., p. 70.

CHAPTER 5

1. Kissane, *The Irish Famine*, p. 109.
2. Ibid., p. 97.
3. Ibid., p. 120.
4. Ibid., p. 110.

CHAPTER 6

1. Kissane, *The Irish Famine*, p. 80.
2. Ibid., p. 124.

3. Donnelly, *The Great Irish Potato Famine*, p. 79.
4. Ibid., p. 92.

CHAPTER 7
1. Kissane, *The Irish Famine*, p. 159.
2. Ibid., p. 165.

CHAPTER 8
1. Donnelly, *The Great Irish Potato Famine*, p. 130.
2. Ibid., p. 127.
3. Ibid., p. 96.
4. Ibid., p. 97.
5. Ibid., p. 111.
6. Ibid., p. 144.
7. Kissane, *The Irish Famine*, p. 140.
8. Helen Litton, *The Irish Famine: An Illustrated History*, 2nd edition. Dublin: Wolfhound Press, 2003, p. 98.

CHAPTER 9
1. Litton, *The Irish Famine*, p. 116.
2. Donnelly, *The Great Irish Potato Famine*, p. 205.

3. Ibid., pp. 204–205.
4. Litton, *The Irish Famine*, p. 118.
5. Donnelly, *The Great Irish Potato Famine*, p. 26.
6. Ibid., p. 166.
7. Kissane, *The Irish Famine*, p. 178.
8. Litton, *The Irish Famine*, p. 129.
9. Donnelly, *The Great Irish Potato Famine*, color plates, p. 7.
10. Ibid.

CHAPTER 10
1. Donnelly, *The Great Irish Potato Famine*, p. 23.
2. Ibid., pp. 210–211.
3. Kissane, *The Irish Famine*, p. 174.
4. Donnelly, *The Great Irish Potato Famine*, p. 210.
5. Ibid., p. 17.
6. Ibid., p. 121.
7. Kathy Marks, "Blair Issues Apology for Irish Potato Famine," *The Independent*, June 2, 1997. http://www.independent.co.uk/news/blair-issues-apology-for-irish-potato-famine-1253790.html.
8. Ibid.

BIBLIOGRAPHY

Donnelly, James S. Jr. *The Great Irish Potato Famine.* Stroud, Gloucestershire: Sutton, 2001.

Gribben, Arthur, ed. *The Great Famine and the Irish Diaspora in America.* Amherst: University of Massachusetts Press, 1999.

Kinealy, Christine. *This Great Calamity: The Irish Famine, 1845–52.* Boulder, Colo.: Roberts Rinehart, 1995.

Kissane, Noel. *The Irish Famine: A Documentary History.* Dublin: National Library of Ireland, 1995.

Litton, Helen. *The Irish Famine: An Illustrated History.* 2nd edition. Dublin: Wolfhound Press, 2003.

Ó Gráda, Cormac. *Black '47 and Beyond: The Great Irish Famine.* Princeton, N.J.: Princeton University Press, 1999.

Tóibin, Colm, and Diarmaid Ferriter. *The Irish Famine: A Documentary.* New York: St. Martin's Press, 2002.

FURTHER RESOURCES

BOOKS

Bartoletti, Susan Campbell. *Black Potatoes: The Story of the Great Irish Famine, 1845–1850*. Boston: Houghton Mifflin, 2001.

Gray, Peter. *The Irish Famine*. New York: H.N. Abrams, 1995.

Hogan, Edward Patrick, and Erin Hogan Fouberg. *Ireland*. New York: Chelsea House, 2003.

Hoobler, Dorothy and Thomas. *The Irish American Family Album*. New York: Oxford University Press, 1995.

O'Neill, Joseph R. *The Irish Potato Famine*. Edina, Minn.: Abdo Publishing, 2009.

Price Hossell, Karen. *The Irish Americans*. San Diego: Lucent Books, 2003.

WEB SITES

Irish Catholic Immigration to America
http://www.loc.gov/teachers/classroommaterials/presentationsandactivities/presentations/immigration/irish2.html

The Irish Famine
http://www.bbc.co.uk/history/british/victorians/famine_01.shtml

Irish Views of the Famine
http://xroads.virginia.edu/~hyper/SADLIER/IRISH/Irish.htm

Views of the Famine
http://adminstaff.vassar.edu/sttaylor/FAMINE

PICTURE CREDITS

INDEX

A

Achill Island, 94
Act for the Temporary Relief
 of the Destitute Persons in
 Ireland, 64
Act of Union, 90, 102–103
American Indians, 59
Anglicans, 94
Anglo-Irish Treaty, 103
Archill Island, 22
Atlantic Ocean crossings, 71–75
Australia, 71, 90, 92, 107

B

bacillus dysentery, 51
Ballingarry, Battle of, 91
bankruptcy, 95
Barrett family, 8–10
Bennett, William, 60–61
black fever, 51, 56–57
Blair, Tony, 107
blight, origins and cause of,
 30–32
bloody flux, 51
Board of Works, 44, 45–48, 63
bobbies, 29
Bradley, Michael, 81
British Association for the Relief
 of the Extreme Distress in
 Ireland and Scotland, 58–59
Bruton, John, 107
Byrne, Gabriel, 107

C

Canada, 59, 71–75, 108
Catholics, 40, 42–43, 76, 85, 94
Central Board of Health, 57
Central Relief Committee of
 the Society of Friends, 59–63

charities, 36, 58–63, 91, 94
Choctaw Nation, 59
cholera, 94–95
Citizen (newspaper), 92
civil service reform, 43
Clonakilty, 11, 12
coal, 20
coffin ships, 72–73
commemorations, 106–107
Connacht, 100
Cork, 33
corn, 13, 32–37, 44, 50
Corn Laws, 32–33, 37
corruption, 46
County Clare, 34–35, 87
credit, 47
Creedon, J., 13–14
Crime and Outrage Act, 87
Crimean War, 65
crop failures, previous, 26, 28
curl, 26
Custom House Quays, 107, 108

D

De Vere, Stephen, 72–73
deaths, statistics on, 17, 100
Diary of a Dispensary Doctor
 (Donovan), 8
Dickens, Charles, 22
diseases (crop), 26
diseases (human), 50–57, 71,
 75, 94–95, 100
Donaghmore Famine
 Workhouse Museum, 107
Donovan, Daniel, 8–10, 13
Doonass, 34–35
Dorian, Hugh, 48–49
dropsy, 50
dry rot, 26

ABOUT THE AUTHOR

LIZ SONNEBORN is a writer who lives in Brooklyn, New York. A graduate of Swarthmore College, she has written more than 80 books for children, young adults, and adults. Her works include *The End of Apartheid in South Africa*, *The American West*, *The California Gold Rush*, *A to Z of American Indian Women*, *The Great Black Migrations*, and *The Ancient Kushites*, which the African Studies Association's Children's Africana Book Awards named an Honor Book for Older Readers in 2006.